FROM THE MOUSE'S HOUSE TO THE PENTHOUSE

From the Mouse's House *to the* Penthouse

What I Learned from Making Deals,
Building Brands, and Running Businesses in Asia

Michael Crawford

Former Senior Executive at Disney and Four Seasons Hotels

LIONCREST
PUBLISHING

FROM THE MOUSE'S HOUSE TO THE PENTHOUSE
What I Learned from Making Deals, Building Brands, and Running Businesses in Asia

FIRST EDITION

ISBN   978-1-5445-4184-6   *Hardcover*
        978-1-5445-4183-9   *Paperback*
        978-1-5445-4182-2   *Ebook*
        978-1-5445-4185-3   *Audiobook*

Dedicated to my incredible daughter Kaitlin Crawford, who inspires and drives me every day to want to be better so she has a father she can be proud of always! While I was out doing deals around the world, all you wanted for Christmas from Santa was for "Daddy to be home more." You and me, kid! Thank you for being born, and for being my Monka!!

Contents

INTRODUCTION 9

1. THE BUSINESS OF BUSINESS 25

2. DOING WHAT'S RIGHT FOR THE MARKET 39

3. RESPECT THE CULTURE 77

4. THE ART OF NEGOTIATION 95

5. ON THE GROUND 143

6. WORKING IN ASIA 179

CONCLUSION 207

ACKNOWLEDGMENTS... 211

ABOUT THE AUTHOR 213

\

Introduction

The day I boarded the airplane to move to Tokyo in 2001 years ago with my wife and young daughter, I was scared to death. I'd only been there once before, for four days, a fog of jet lag during which I'd met the team I'd be leading, found an apartment for us to live in, ordered a whole houseful of furniture, and enrolled my daughter in a school.

Now I could barely even remember which neighborhood I'd picked to live in.

So I sat on the plane feeling less excited about my new job and more terrified about what I'd gotten into.

None of us slept much on the flight, so we arrived exhausted, but at least there was a man at the airport holding a sign with our name on it. He drove us to the apartment. All the furniture was in place, and there was food, soap, towels. There were even two cell phones, one for me and one for my wife, and a car downstairs in the garage. That was reassuring.

I didn't sleep more than an hour that night from a combination of nerves and jet lag. In the morning, Sunday, I let the others sleep and had the brilliant idea of learning how to drive our new right-hand drive car.

I was soon driving around in a cold sweat trying to figure out how to get back to our new home. Tokyo is a complicated city. It's not on a grid system. It has lots of alleyways and small streets, and everyone just parks in the street with the blinkers on while they do their business. And there are no street signs.

I didn't have my cell phone. Not that I had anyone to call. My wife wouldn't be able to help, and she was asleep anyway.

After about three hours, I finally recognized a street and found my way back.

I realized over the next couple of years that I'd probably never been more than a couple of blocks from the apartment, but it felt much farther. And the feeling of bewilderment stuck with me. It was like going back to being a child who doesn't really understand how anything works.

That's the thing about other cultures. They can be disorientating. And intriguing. And exciting. All at once.

* * *

Three years later, I was sitting at a blackjack table in Las Vegas when I was offered an opportunity to become part of a new international business development team for the Parks & Resorts Division of the Walt Disney Company that would end up with me leading the deal to build the Shanghai Disney Resort—Disney's first theme park in mainland China, and its biggest overseas investment anywhere.

By then, I was a far more savvy expat...but my time in Tokyo was up. I was preparing to move back to Florida, to take up a new role at Disney MGM Studios. It was always a good idea to get back in the swing of operations in the United States. In virtually any global company, people who go overseas on assignment risk being seen as parked up and left behind. Or, if they make sure to communicate enough with the mothership, they get exposure. That's what happened to me.

One of my last acts in Japan was to start discussing a deal with Cirque du Soleil for a new show at Tokyo Disney Resort, and the executive who had just been appointed to create Disney's new international development team sat in on negotiations. We clicked, and he asked if he could sit in on the next round of meetings, in Las Vegas.

We were playing blackjack at the end of a day of negotiations when he said, "I could really use someone like you on my team. You have operational experience, you have international experience, you've done deals domestically, you've operated with new experiences and different geographies. I think you're just the sort of person who could really help the company if you came into business development."

My wife was expecting my next job to be at Walt Disney World Resort in Orlando, where we still had a home. Instead I called her from the Las Vegas Strip and said, "How about this opportunity to move to California and work for new business development?"

Mike flanked by dragons to mark Chinese New Year in Singapore.

At the time, Disney was focusing on expanding into key international geographies by building new theme park and resort experiences. I'd been there and done that, and had been successful. It was a case of right place, right time. So I agreed and became one of Disney's international deal makers.

Disney had recently built a resort in Hong Kong. In 2004, they sent me to Shanghai to lead the business development team on the deal to build the first Disney property in mainland China. Talks went pretty slowly for a couple of years. Then the Shanghai government was rocked by allegations of corruption and negotiations simply stopped. Everyone forgot us while they rushed to try to clean up their own mess.

Disney asked me to lead new deal teams in Singapore and Malaysia, which were both important gateway countries that would have exposed the company to places with large numbers of what were termed "income-qualified" people—people with enough money to visit Disney—such as India, Southeast Asia, and Australia.

Neither destination happened, for different reasons. Singapore was investigating encouraging international tourism by legalizing gambling, and that wasn't something Disney was happy to sit alongside in terms of sustainable growth. And Malaysia was the wrong shape. Access to the southern part of the country, where we were looking to build, just wasn't good enough.

I was zero for two in my new business development career when the Chinese government announced in late 2007 that they were ready to restart negotiations in Shanghai. But that zero stood for a lot. I'd earned it with a lot of exposure to all parts of deal development, process management, and key lessons about working in different markets. I sat down and did an assessment of what had worked for me as a deal lead in Singapore and Malaysia, compared with my previous experience in Shanghai, and I came to a conclusion.

I asked Disney if I could lead the deal team in Shanghai. I asked them to let me pick a team, go out there, and try an approach that was different from the one we had been using before. I thought we could make a deal.

And, after a lot of meetings, I think Disney management thought, "Nothing we've done to date has worked anyways. What do we have to lose?"

I was thinking along the same lines. I've always been motivated by challenges, and trying to achieve something that had failed for two decades was a huge driver for me. Unlike Disney, however, I had something to lose. I'd put my head on the block. In career terms, the deal was make or break.

* * *

The Shanghai Disney Resort deal was one of Disney's biggest company priorities at the time. CEO Bob Iger made it clear it was one of his keys to success for Disney, which was international growth. Expansion in mainland China was critical for all Disney's business verticals. The company would gain access to a new audience of over a billion people who in a changing China were going to have the income to spend on Disney product.

Most people think they understand how to do business in East Asia. It's not new, after all. US companies have been trading in China for decades since the first special economic zones were established to attract direct foreign investment in the 1980s. In Japan, US investment has an even longer history.

A whole subculture of thought leadership has developed around doing business with East Asia, with books and courses for business people thinking about making deals there. Some of the quirky etiquette—not finishing your whole plate of food in China, taking and receiving gifts in Japan—became so well known in America that it was almost a cliche. The general attitude seemed to be that if you were just ready to observe a few odd customs, the Asian market was ready and waiting, crying out for US goods and services.

Modern buildings in Shanghai reflect China's rapid emergence as one of the world's top economic powers.

Of course, the market was vast, thanks largely to the growing economic power of China, which has been steadily creating a larger middle class with more money to spend, more leisure time during which to spend it, and increasingly aspirational lifestyles.

So, thousands of North American businesses sent their representatives out to Asia clutching the business cards they'd learned were essential for meetings and acutely aware of the need to shake hands with the other side in the correct order of seniority. These were the boots on the ground in the campaign to open a vast market to North America. And yet time after time, they failed. They fell afoul of Communist Party bureaucracy or obstructionism, or simply discovered an absence of demand for the products or services they were offering.

Instead of advice on what to wear for business meetings in China—a formal business suit, by the way, without exception—the press started to fill up with articles on how companies doing business there could protect their intellectual property from being cloned by unscrupulous Chinese businesses or how they could get their money back to the United States.

Now people who headed to China weren't just armed with business cards. They were armed with a whole new defensive attitude based on the assumption that the Chinese were about to bushwhack them.

Some were bushwhacked, all right. Most weren't. But very few found the streets paved with gold. And even those who did didn't find it easy.

There's money in China for businesses who get their approach right, but it's a misconception that all a business has to do is set up there and the cash will rain in.

The fact is that there's no such thing as a quick buck in China.

No amount of business cards, hand shaking, and late night drinking is going to change that. You have to do it to show respect, but it's not how business development gets done.

Most Westerners who set out to do business in East Asia tend to see it either as a land of milk and honey where riches will fall in their laps or as a kind of Wild West frontier threatened by bandits and gunfighters. Both views are wrong.

East Asia, and China specifically, does indeed offer opportunity, but it is also a highly competitive, if somewhat undeveloped, market. It is home to 1.6 billion people, a fifth of the planet's population, many of whom are among the first generations in their families to have disposable income. But the key to doing business there is not the order you give out presents in a meeting or the toasts you make at a working dinner. The key is to understand two things about how the people on the other side of the table think and what permission they need to get from senior levels of the government to do business with you.

First, it's very different from you. And second, it's not better or worse. It's just different.

That's what I've brought away from nearly a decade in Asia as an executive of two global brands, The Walt Disney Company and

Four Seasons Hotels and Resorts. I spent four years at Four Seasons, first as President of Asia Pacific for Four Seasons Hotels, and then as Global President of Portfolio Management. Before that, I spent nearly 25 years at Disney, originally in the United States but eventually in Tokyo for three years as Managing Director of Operations of Tokyo Disney Resort, and then as a senior executive in International Development for the Theme Parks & Resorts Division of the Walt Disney Company, charged with the mission of extending Disney experiences around the world...the biggest of which was to get a new deal to build a destination resort in Shanghai, China.

The Shanghai deal had been in the works as long as I'd been at Disney before I got a crack at leading the deal. It took my team years more of negotiation with the local government, the regional government, the national government, and ultimately the Chinese Communist Party. We had to educate our Chinese partners in everything about designing, building, and running a theme park, while in return we had to accommodate their attitudes toward purchasing land (you can't), the legal code (they follow their own), and finance (they have their own banks—and you will use them).

Like I say, there's no such thing as a quick buck in China.

During the process we had meetings with government officials about the development and construction process in China. They asked us many, many questions about how much we were spending, how many workers we would need on site, and how long the build would take.

It turned out that someone from the development department was listening very carefully, writing everything down, and doing calculations. At the end of the discussions, he said, "I've calculated, and according to what you say a project like this is entitled to have this many deaths and this many injuries."

For a moment I thought there was some sort of translation issue. But it turned out that the Chinese had determined a formula to figure out expected casualties on a project. If it came in fewer, no problems.

It was one of the most astounding lessons I had from our Chinese partners.

We said politely, "Our goal is to have no one getting hurt or dying. We'll work with you to create the safest working environment we can."

Some of the Chinese chuckled and shook their heads, like, "Oh, you dumb Americans. You don't know what you're talking about."

But we did. Of all companies, Disney couldn't afford to be associated with casualties building a resort. Imagine the headlines. We told the Chinese, "Safety is not our exclusive IP, it's something we will share with you. We will educate you. We will give you the playbook for safe construction. We want everybody to be alive and safe, whether they're working for us or somebody else."

And that's what happened.

A representative safety warning from a Chinese construction site.

* * *

Old habits die hard. Even today, if I'm walking along the street and I see a piece of litter, I have to pick it up. That's something I learned at Disney over thirty years ago. Any employee walking through a Disney park who sees a piece of trash is trained to pick it up and put it in the trash can.

I love Disney. I first walked into Disney in early 1990 as an hourly employee for three months between my undergraduate studies and my graduate studies. At that time, Disney was expanding like crazy. It was just building Euro Disney in Paris.

I fell in love with what the company stood for in the very first week. That was an incredible five full days at Disney University learning about what they call Disney Traditions. I called my mother on the Friday I graduated and told her, "What a remarkable company that invests this much in teaching people about their culture and who they are."

A couple of months later I called her to tell her I wouldn't be going to grad school. Disney wanted me to stay, and promised to pay for my MBA later, so I went into their management program.

I stayed for nearly twenty-five years. I went from putting on a polyester costume to sell tickets at Disney Pleasure Island in Florida to leading the deal to create Shanghai Disney Resort, the first Disney theme park in mainland China.

Mike on the balcony of the Shanghai Disneyland Hotel, with the completed park behind him.

I never intended to leave, and I would not have done so were it not that the Four Seasons Hotel and Resort Company offered me a chance to create new experiences and build a whole new career path, leveraging things I had learned from Disney and on my own living internationally for almost a decade.

And I still never walk past a piece of litter without picking it up.

* * *

This isn't a book about Disney or about Four Seasons. It's a book about what I learned from making international deals and running company divisions for two of the biggest branded companies in the world. I've sat across the table from local partners, national governments, global brands, and the Chinese Communist Party and come away with the best results I could. I've led teams tasked with making deals so complex and challenging that even the people who hired me were surprised when they succeeded. I've lived on other continents and in different cultures. I've overcome resistance not only from the other side of the table but also from my own side, from dubious members of my own team to wary head offices and admin departments on the other side of the world.

I've been in the room when monolithic cultures have clashed and I've figured out a way to find common ground so that they both give enough to satisfy the other but not so much that they're disappointed for themselves. No one wins and no one loses: they share a negotiation.

On the way, I learned a lot about doing deals around the world, particularly in East Asia and the Pacific.

That's what this book is about. Shanghai Disney Resort was the highest-profile deal I was involved in, not just for its cost and complexity, but also for its symbolic importance. Disney on the one hand as a standard-bearer of Western commerce and US values—remember that Mickey Mouse was identified as a metaphor for Western cultural imperialism back in the 1960s and 1970s—and monolithic Chinese communism on the other. The media eagerly tracked the deal, as did governments and businesses around the world. I'm proud of what my team and I accomplished. We still gather now and then to celebrate the achievement. But if you want to read a blow-by-blow account of the creation of Shanghai Disney Resort, you'll have to find another book.

This isn't an insider story of the deal. It's not a book about the specifics of individual negotiations. Instead, it uses the deals I've been involved in as the basis for a set of general principles. Those principles will be useful for doing business anywhere—I learned many of them in California and Florida, the twin poles of the Disney world in North America—but particularly in Asia and the Pacific, and probably most of all in China.

Western companies keep getting it wrong in China. They go there with unrealistic expectations. They go with blinders on that prevent them from seeing that business doesn't happen there in the same way it does in North America. They go worrying about imaginary problems and failing to address the very real ones.

As I'm about to show you, it doesn't have to be that way. By applying a set of principles, it's possible to prepare yourself in a way that will increase your chances of success.

This book is your manual. This book is your due diligence. This book is how you make sure that when you walk into the room for the first time you know what's about to happen.

And it's got nothing to do with business cards, shaking hands, or gifts.

CHAPTER 1

The Business of Business

UNDERSTAND YOUR PARTNER

The key conversations take place outside the meetings when you forge relationships with people you can get on your side.

Business depends on trust. That means it takes time, because trust in any relationship takes time. It takes even longer when you represent a large, internationally-branded corporation with a strong culture and your counterparts are a part of the Communist Party machinery, as my counterparts were during the deal for Shanghai Disney Resort. But it's still possible to become culturally and personally aligned with the people you're doing business with, because they have the same investment in success as you. The need for trust means that big deals aren't quick—but if you get them right, they're also going to be a marriage of cultures that will last for decades. My counterparts and I had to figure out a way to be successful together—or we would both look bad.

HONEST CONVERSATIONS START WITH TRUST

Sometimes in China, you'd go into the room for high-level negotiations and a bunch of faceless bureaucrats would turn up. You don't know who they are, you've never seen them before, and they're not introduced. It sounds intimidating—and it can be, a little—but ultimately it's irrelevant. Whoever they are, they're not important. The important people are your counterparts on the deal team, the people you go to drinks with or eat dinner with. The key conversations take place outside the meetings when you forge relationships with people you can get on on your side. They become your advocates who will share their positions with you: "Look, I can take this to Shanghai, Beijing, or whatever. And this is what I can probably do. And in return this is what *you* will have to do."

You get to that position by going to lunches, eating dinners, sharing drinks. We would go on day trips together to see other hotels or various visitor attractions. You have to sit down and spend quality time with the other side. After a while, the teams build close relationships and start exchanging gifts for meaningful events. We came to understand that the only way the deal was going to get done was to have deep and honest discussions, even if they were sometimes painful and awkward. For that you need trust—and for that you need to build relationships.

BRING YOUR PARTNERS INTO THE PROCESS

If you can get the Chinese working alongside you, your chances of success are much, much higher. You don't just need them on board. You have to make them part of your team.

Disney usually did business in a way that was uncommon anywhere in the world, let alone in communist China, because of the power of its brand. In past Disney deals, governments were more than willing to provide subsidy, land, tax forgiveness, and other concessions to incentivize a world-class brand to take up residency and drive profile and economic value to their particular geography. But China wasn't going to be the same. There was a lot we had to change in order to have credibility at the deal table and make the partnership work for the long term. You could go down the route of setting up a wholly foreign-owned enterprise (WFOE), but that means you have to do everything for yourself—but every other company I consulted with about this told me it would be foolish. Anyone doing business in China needs the government on its side on many fronts to help with regulatory issues, licensing, infrastructure, and everything else.

The handover ceremony as Shanghai Shendi takes charge of the Chinese side of the project.

The choice is to bring your partners into the tent so that you share the costs and they have some input and oversight. The Chinese set up a state-owned entity named Shanghai Shendi (Group) Co., Ltd., to partner with Disney, and the head of Shanghai Shendi became chairman of our board. The government wanted even more control, because whatever they do is heavily scrutinized, but they settled for a seat on the board.

Disney was learning the difference between doing business in mainland China against doing business in Hong Kong, say, or other parts of the world. I told them, "Let me show you what companies typically invest when they start a business in China. They increase their risk profile, but if they don't do it, the Chinese will not allow them any control."

My strategy was to look at how other high-profile companies were handling Chinese requests and negotiating guardrails around equal risk and control. I put together a pretty compelling set of business and qualitative reasons around why the deal would make sense—but if we didn't put up more finance, there was no reason for the Chinese to negotiate. It was a linchpin item for them. The Chinese understood that we wanted creative control and operational control, but they wanted to be alongside us, which is why they set up Shanghai Shendi.

We went back to the drawing board and looked at what other companies had invested to gain credibility. We saw there was room to maneuver, but we wanted to keep our know-how, so there was no knowledge-transfer agreement, and we had a very protective license agreement between the Walt Disney Company and Shanghai Disney to license the Disney brand.

Just because the Chinese were our partners didn't mean they could just decide one day to go out and give Mickey a completely new hat. No one in the world gets to do that outside Disney.

BE AWARE OF OTHERS' PERSPECTIVE OF THE UNITED STATES

Years of working abroad have given me a different perspective on how people from the United States are perceived while doing business or running companies. Non-Americans are wary of what they see as a US-centric approach. You need to beware of falling into the trap of assuming that everything we do in the States is the best and most advanced way of doing it. Instead, it's smart business to listen and learn first, so you can merge the best from both geographies. Sometimes, another country wants the technology or support of the United States, in which case making deals is easy. But if the other country feels as advanced as the States, you need to be more nuanced in how you deal with them.

It's not easy for companies that have had success on their own to set aside their egos for the sake of the team. But that's exactly why the most successful sports superstars like Michael Jordan and Tom Brady *are* superstars—because they know they're only one part of a team and they've got the mentality to work with others to achieve the same goal. If just one individual on a deal team sees negotiation in terms of a personal victory, it can disrupt the entire chemistry of the team doing the deal.

It can be difficult. For some Americans, the perception of the United States as always being right is sometimes the biggest hurdle to working with overseas partners—and at home. Meanwhile, in some parts of the world there is a perception that the United States is trying to impose its culture everywhere, so people are wary of US businesses. The businesses that do better anywhere are those that can take a step back and see challenges through a wide lens.

Every country has its national pride, and they want to know you're not just dumping American culture on them at the cost of their own. That was particularly true of Disney. The *Wall Street Journal* said that Shanghai Disney would be like an aircraft carrier for US culture to China.

It was interesting that things weren't the same with Four Seasons. No one worries about Canadian culture like they do about US culture. Canada is like Switzerland: no one sees it as a threat. Canadians are gentle socialists who don't get into wars. Canada is an easy country to go to and an easy country to leave.

No one ever had a demonstration to keep Canadian products out of their country.

GLOBALIZATION LEAVES ROOM FOR NUANCE

It's common to hear a lot of concern about how globalization will eventually make everything the same in every place around the world: what's known as Starbuckization. I'm pretty sanguine about the idea, because the negative view ignores the obvious nuance. A Starbucks in China is slightly different from a Starbucks in Seattle, and both are different from a Starbucks in Britain.

Truly successful global companies understand the difference

between products at home and abroad, and how they both relate to the brand. When you travel from the United States to Spain, or Germany, or Singapore, and you see the golden arches outside a burger restaurant, you know what's inside. It's dependable. You walk in because you know you can get fries, a Coke or Pepsi, and a hamburger. But then you get inside in Japan and you can have a Big Mac or you can have a teriyaki burger with an egg on it. Or a McSpicy Paneer in India. Those are authentic local twists you don't come across in the United States.

Global companies accept that learning is a 360-degree premise. Trends can start from anywhere in the world. When I traveled to Hawaii and visited a high-end burger place, they had a burger made from Japanese Wagyu beef and you could add an egg to it. That never existed in the United States until someone went to Japan, saw how popular it was, and tried it. They decided that it might not be time for eggs on burgers in North America just yet, but they positioned it as a specialty burger and believed that people would like it. Now eggs are on burgers everywhere.

The goal in running a company internationally, or in negotiating a deal internationally, is to remain open to these influences. Don't draw hard lines on a map and say, "Our product can only evolve here." You need to leave room for cross-pollination of great product or service ideas, no matter where they originate from.

A Coca-Cola in China still has its red can with a pop top, and it still has brown sugar water, but it has a slightly different taste. It's marketed differently than it is in the United States—but the branding is the same because the Chinese are familiar with it from TV and movies and they don't want to feel that they're being disrespected. They don't want to feel they're getting Coke's second-best.

That's how multinational companies are successful. They create their product in other countries for those countries. And then they take those learnings to other places so that when those customers visit in their home country, the customers feel comfortable having the product there too, even though it might be, say, 20 percent different from what the customers are used to.

THE BIGGER PICTURE

> You can only do business overseas if you can see the bigger picture. It's not just about seeing beyond where you are; you have to see beyond when, too.

Years ago, when Disney decided to put all its content into a new digital ecosystem called iTunes, people said, "What the heck are you doing? You won't be able to sell DVDs or video tapes." But Disney understood that was not where people were going to live anymore. They were going to live in a world where they didn't have to be at home or in a movie theater for three hours to watch a movie. Disney saw that people wanted mobility, control, and a tailored experience. They didn't mind paying, but they wanted to be able to watch the same sort of content without interruption wherever they were. They wanted personalization. That's what Blockbuster got wrong. Blockbuster thought people wanted access to video tapes, but people wanted access to content. They didn't care how it was delivered.

Disney saw how technology was going to develop and how it would give individuals the opportunity to create their own content. That presaged the rise of social media, and the fact that younger people today like seeing real people talk about things that relate to their own lives. It doesn't feel like a commercial. It feels like insider information. Today companies leverage that content. They tell influencers, "Go use our product like you would in everyday life. Talk about it. Make content about it." So the influencers pick up that box of Tide or that can of Coke and say, "Man, this is fantastic. This makes my life feel so much better."

If you're Disney or Four Seasons now, you give influencers access to your content and they become your marketing people. You trust them to know better what's going on in people's lives, so they can come up with things that are truly inclusive.

Disney has been doing that for years. Disney came up with a brilliant marketing campaign in the 2000s that showed families surprising their kids on Christmas morning with a trip to Disney. The people filmed it themselves and Disney edited together a collection that brought tears to your eyes. The slogan was, "What are you going to celebrate?" They'd show a ninety-year-old grandpa having a birthday party down at Disney and the family surprising him, or a same-sex couple walking down Main Street when gay marriage had just been legalized. The idea was, "We want to be a part of what you're doing in your life."

That's where companies that develop an international strategy are really successful. They want to be a part of people's lives—and that means your product or service has to be relevant to *them*, not to *you*. They want to have their own selection ready to watch rather than what has been programmed on TV by a bunch of strangers or a computer.

The world has changed. Fashion once started in Paris and made its way across the world. Not anymore. Now it comes from all over. Nothing comes from a single source. Not everyone wants to visit Sleeping Beauty's castle in California; they expect to see a castle closer to home.

ENTERING A MARKET IS ALSO ABOUT BUILDING YOUR BRAND

Four Seasons has many similarities with Disney. It has cult status, and people who engage with its products become followers. It's not cheap, but once you've got people to stay and they've felt what the service is like and how the environment reflects local customs and cultures, that starts to build loyalty toward that brand.

The hook is usually food and beverage. People come in for a meal or a drink and they see the beautiful hotel. They see the level of service. Then, when they travel to India or Vietnam, or Singapore, they're looking for the same hotel. That's what Four Seasons wants.

It was the same with Disney. They didn't build Shanghai Disney just to be successful in China. They wanted to build brand loyalty in the huge, emerging Chinese middle class. If Chinese travelers went to California, they had to go to Disneyland. If they went to Florida, they had to go to Walt Disney World Resort. If they went to Paris, they had to see Disneyland Resort Paris.

Companies need to consider how doing business internationally builds a much broader customer base around the world. People carry the idea of the brand around the world. If I drive a Ford in my home country and I go to a rental car office abroad, what vehicle do you think I'm asking for? So it's vital that businesses achieve consistency of products or services to develop their loyal customers—but they can still introduce surprising twists that turn up in local cultures.

Companies sometimes think about international growth as simply expanding what they do in North America to other places. But a savvy company realizes that the process is not one way. It's a round trip. Sure, you're taking what you do here over there, but you'd be a fool if you didn't also bring what you do over there back here. You take advantage of lessons from other countries to grow your business at home because you know those consumers travel outside of their home countries. If you build loyalty where they live, you can expect them to stay with you when they travel or move to live somewhere else.

DON'T BE AFRAID TO ADAPT YOUR PRODUCT

Every day a company starts that does something better than anyone else. The company has so much success it comes to believe that no one else will ever do it better than them. They convince themselves they cannot change how they work. They become unwilling to evolve their product or service. "Why do I need to change this if it's successful? You're asking me to dilute my brand." Someone might say, "The world's a small place. If the guests who use my soap in Ohio go to London and buy my soap and it's different there, I risk losing that guest because they've built trust with what I do."

Some brands hold very tight to that, but it's a delusion. Others understand the truth, which is that you have to nuance the taste or the smell or the feel of your product, or the speed or cost of your service, depending on where you're doing business.

THINK LIKE A STARTUP

When a business goes into a new territory, it has to go back to the mentality of being a startup—because that's effectively what it is. That's true even of businesses that have been around the best part of a century, like Disney.

The world is full of people judging every step a business takes: analysts, Wall Street, investors, the board. That makes it a defensible position for a business to go into a new country and keep doing what they normally do. That's brought them success and made them money. It's easier to tell the Board that you're going to do what you did before than to tell them you're going to do something completely different to make it more relevant to the particular market. But remember when your business started in the United States: you had to be flexible as you learned the market.

Ford didn't start rolling trucks off the assembly line and become profitable on day one. It had to develop its marketing, sell some trucks, and stabilize the business. Companies working overseas today want to skip those steps. They think, "This is what works. This is how we market it. This is how we build it. This is how we put it out to the market."

But a new market needs time and research. First to market isn't always best to market. Sometimes first follower or second follower is not a bad position to be in. You can see and learn from the mistakes others are making so that you can be successful quicker.

You don't have to turn up fully fledged. From the time Disney signed the deal for Shanghai it took about six or seven years to open the resort. That wasn't just because of the construction work. We were also learning how to operate in China, how to become culturally relevant to the Chinese, and how to market that relevance to our potential customers.

The Shanghai site, cleared and ready for building.

An overview of the Shanghai site at the start of construction.

My presence in Shanghai made things easier because I had operational experience. It's a tough call for businesses timing the switch-over from the development team to the operating team. No one wants to send operating people or hire a local operating team in a destination before there is anything to operate—but if you leave it too late, the operators don't get a chance to give any meaningful input into the development.

The fact that I was involved gave us operating-team continuity from the time the deal was signed until the day the front gate was opened. I was learning the culture, building relationships, and educating Disney to accept that things were going to be different in Shanghai than elsewhere. Otherwise those things would not have happened until after Shanghai Disney opened.

For everyone, though, this is a situation where the Gantt chart tells you one thing about how teams succeed one another, but it's more important simply to make sure that there's overlap and synchronicity between all the teams. It might cost a bit more, but it saves realizations late in the game that might end up costing a whole lot more.

CHAPTER 2

Doing What's Right for the Market

Making the decision to do deals overseas is one thing in a boardroom in North America, and another thing completely when you're boots on the ground in an unfamiliar environment, with different sights, sounds, and experiences. A line in a business plan can't prepare people for the reality of working in another culture. Looking at a world map or reading books is not the same as being immersed in the geography and being surrounded by those who live and do business there.

A lot of multinational companies have regional headquarters in Africa and the Middle East, Asia Pacific, the Americas, Europe, and Latin America. Those headquarters have all the usual specialists with their own expertise, but everywhere is different. An accountant headquartered in Paris doesn't know everything about taxation in every country in Europe.

Four Seasons brought me in to help grow their Asia office in Singapore. Their employees there and the business owners were eager to have more expertise on the ground to understand the different cultures in that time zone. They wanted to triple growth in China and knew that they needed additional resources to support it. It was the same for Disney. When you make a strategic priority of entering into a specific country, invest there at least until you figure out all the nuances to doing business there. Once the company or entity is operating, you can determine whether all the resources you have already brought in are necessary for the long term. You might be able to refine your operation and combine it with other entities. You might be able to outsource some of it. It's important to make those decisions once you've got the boots on the ground to make a proper assessment.

UNDERSTANDING THE MARKET

To do business anywhere with credibility, you have to have a team that's empowered and that has residency.

Shanghai was exactly the right place for Disney to build a resort because it has become an international destination for tourism and business. It had the wealth to sustain a massive project where we were going to charge to get in, to get food, and to buy merchandise. It was the only choice. Beijing was too close to the government, with the Central Committee and everything else communism stood for.

When the Chinese started traveling in numbers back in the 1990s, they concentrated on wonder and beauty, usually meaning national monuments and natural parks. But soon visiting Tokyo to shop in the Ginza or visiting Paris to shop became high on the list of reasons to travel. People had read about the Eiffel

Tower, say, or other well-known tourist destinations, but Disney parks and other amusement parks were not high on their list.

The concept of a theme park didn't exist in China. Their style of amusement park has a random collection of rides, like a fairground. There's no immersion into a themed world. They just go ride a rollercoaster. A lot of learning needed to occur from a government and partner point of view. They didn't understand the concept of upkeep and maintenance. They didn't know how to reinvest in adding new attractions, or how to market a destination.

LOCALIZE YOUR APPROACH TO THE MARKET

When Disney built its first owned and operated overseas park, Euro Disney in Paris (now Disneyland Resort Paris), it was a new experience for the company. Tokyo Disney Resort had been owned and operated by someone else—an Asian lessee—who adapted the Disney brand to Japanese culture.

In Paris, Disney believed the formula for success was really more about domestic business and regional European business. A lot of French and other Europeans were already going to Walt Disney World Resort in Florida in large numbers, so , Disney felt that it had an understanding of their preferences—though like most companies, they understood that when they actually built the park in Paris they would clearly have to adapt and evolve to that particular location.

Kaitlin Crawford visits Space Mountain at Disneyland Resort, Paris.

There were things that did not change, however, given Disney's normal MO. As an example, the park in Florida was alcohol free, so they opened the park in France without alcohol, too. That was a miss, given the culture in France. When the French came to America and they visited Walt Disney World Resort, they didn't expect to have a glass of wine. They may not have been happy about it, but they understood that was how America worked. But in their own country, they didn't understand that at all. When you take American brands or any country's brands into a different geography, you have to try to figure out how to match your product or service with what their expectations are.

By the time we worked on the Shanghai deal, Disney's approach had evolved not only in the theme park business but also in movies and merchandising. The business model changed. Disney brought in country managers or regional leaders from local ethnicities who could give better cultural perspective and advice. It's easier to hire locally and teach people how to think like your business than it is to teach your business how to think like a local culture.

LOCALIZATION IS A METAPHOR FOR DOING BUSINESS OVERSEAS

Some people simply can't get out of their own routines when they work abroad. They agonize over having to figure out how to use a different laundry detergent than they're used to at home. Others just say, "Who cares what laundry detergent we use? Just get the one everyone uses here."

The laundry detergent is a metaphor for business. When you're in another geography, you can't simply insist, "No, *this* is what we'll do." You have to find the thing that works there. A lot of executives fail around this. They know what it was to be successful one time in a different place, so they try to replicate the same formula as opposed to taking what made them successful and tailoring the product or service for the new geography.

Walt Disney did not start by insisting what Disneyland would be. He started from the premise of creating a place where people can leave their worries behind and immerse themselves in wonderful stories as a family or a couple or a group. That was it. He created a ride called It's a Small World where people traveled in small boats through a water flume, seeing puppets dancing and singing in different national costumes from around the world. The ride showed the unity and beauty of cultures coming together. It showed the universality of children being happy.

That's still the point, giving people a chance to be immersed in an environment they have never seen before. It doesn't matter if it's completely culturally relevant, it doesn't matter if it's not like the ride in California. It just has to give people a chance to go someplace they've never been before.

That's where companies lose the narrative and stick to what they know works. It doesn't always work. Take Kodak. Kodak's philosophy was that people take pictures, pictures are on film, film gets developed, people get a tangible memory they can hold in their hand or put in a frame. They thought the printed photograph was the important thing, but they lost sight of what they were actually trying to do, which was giving people a chance to remember moments and experiences. They didn't understand that no one cares if the memory is on a piece of paper or on a phone.

TAKE TIME TO UNDERSTAND

If you want to do business in a geography, take the time to fully understand what's important there. Companies make mistakes when they're not willing to invest time and education to really see whether their product will fit into a culture or whether they need to evolve it to resonate more with consumers. Coca-Cola would likely have failed if it just presented its regular formula for Coke in China without adjusting the taste for consumers who didn't have such a sweet tooth.

Cultural differences can foil even the smartest plans. Walmart went into Japan and opened the kind of huge superstores that make them so popular in the States. They didn't work. The Japanese didn't have a tradition of buying more cheaply in bulk. Many didn't have room in their homes to store bulk goods, so they tended to have one suit in their closet rather than five, and two pairs of shoes instead of ten. Their quality-over-quantity mindset is evolving now, but at the time it didn't fit with what Walmart offered—and Walmart had to shut all of its Japan stores down.

Every time a new company thinks about going global, they make the same mistake. They start with, "Here's what we do. Here's how we do it. This is what feels good to us—and by gosh, it's going to be successful." Then when it doesn't succeed, they come up with a bunch of excuses: "Maybe the people didn't understand our product. Maybe we had the wrong partner. Maybe it wasn't the right time for us to be there." Management comes up with many ways to justify its strategy, even if it doesn't work. But most of the time, it's the Walmart story again. It's about failing to understand the local way of doing business.

DETERMINE WHICH ROLES NEED TO BE ON THE GROUND AND WHEN

You have to be there—in big enough numbers. Four Seasons's

strategy was for a third of its new hotel inventory to be built in Asia, but the Asia corporate headquarters in Singapore was a small office that needed to grow and evolve to fulfill that mission. It needed to have more business development support and financial support as it created more business. The attorney work was mainly being done from corporate headquarters supported by local consultants. I was brought in as a leader who understood the nuances of doing business in Asia so I could tell them what resources they needed and precisely what those resources would achieve in return for the expense.

Mike visits a potential site for a new Four Seasons hotel in southern Japan with the deal team, potential owner, and architects.

Too many times, people get sent to work overseas and as soon as they get to their new office they pick up the phone to corporate HQ and say, "I need more people." They don't put the right thought into it. They don't give the right quantitative and qualitative justification, so they don't get a return on the investment.

Which only helps to create the perception back at HQ that they've gone rogue and are trying to build an empire, over just saying, "Ah, okay, they need an attorney, they need a financial person, they need a tax person. They need people who understand the laws and regulations from a human resources point of view."

The responsibility goes both ways. The company gives them the opportunity to go and be a part of this culture and understand it. And the individual has the obligation of being able to articulate a compelling story around finances and brand awareness and product evolution in a way that is understandable by the corporate headquarters.

Nobody understood how to think about the brand in the context of Asia—and Asia includes so much variety that it's not really a useful label. Two years later, when I left, we felt far more equipped and prepared for growth with the roles that had been added and support from Four Seasons corporate and the board. It's a mistake to try to do the work with as few people and as cheaply as you can but still hope for big results. That ignores protecting the brand, doing deals, and making sure that legally and financially we were accountable for the goals we had set.

If a company is setting up abroad, or even just in a new town or state at home, it needs to make sure it has people it trusts in the key positions who have the right communication but also a responsibility for finance and for the company's brand. That will ensure that whatever they're setting up can be profitable in the long term but also a part of the fabric of the society where it is.

That helps alleviate some of the frustration, because when you're trying to manage business overseas from a home office in a different time zone, and sometimes a very different time zone, somebody has to be up really early or really late to enable direct communication. That creates frustration for people at home and people on the ground. And then the communication starts to suffer. At both Disney and Four Seasons, our government partners and business partners in Japan, say, or Singapore, would be frustrated with the lack of empowerment because the time difference meant that headquarters was out of the picture and the company didn't have the right resources on the ground to make decisions.

Companies make a mistake by not understanding how frustrating a lack of presence can be for partners. Many of the Four Seasons owners provided me immediate feedback that they would prefer to have more empowered Human Resources located in the Asian markets versus dealing with the time zone challenges when working with key functional leaders from the East Coast of North America. As part of my strategic plan to enhance our business capabilities with culturally sensitized, and time zone relevant employees, I lobbied the Board and Leadership team at Four Seasons to hire more subject matters experts in market, or to move critical new line of business leaders from more established geographies to help grow relationships and make our business development model more effective and efficient. The company agreed given the aggressive growth targets that had been articulated for Asia. With the right talent more centrally located to most of the key priority markets, meetings and visits could be more frequent. This change would create greater trust and could actually cut down on costs of more distant travel. Moreover, the owners then felt they were heard and had individuals who lived in "their part of the world" that had a much better understanding of local cultures, legal environments and more. They could build even closer relationships in a fraction of the time because they were there.

If you don't build relationships, you build no trust, and without trust you don't get the deal done. You don't get the credibility from living in a place, seeing how people there consume a product or service, or how other companies are successful in marketing those products and selling those services. You don't get the credibility from having people there through weekdays and weekends, through big holidays, through difficult political times, experiencing what's going on so that they can evolve the thinking and the level of product or service accordingly.

Mike and his lead interpreter wear Halloween masks designed to be appropriate for Chinese culture.

When I got to Four Seasons, one of the first things I told them was, "To really grow here, one of the first things we need to do is build a team that understands Asia, that has the ability to live there, and that has credibility there."

To do business anywhere with credibility, you have to have a team that's empowered and that has residency. Flying a team in and out won't cut it. It's not efficient. You build no trust. You have no relationships. It won't get the deal done.

VIRTUAL OR LONG-DISTANCE RELATIONSHIP BUILDING IS DIFFICULT

By forcing people into doing business through technology, the pandemic has created a false impression. People concluded that you can do deals just by talking on Zoom, or you can run a company in Bangladesh without ever setting foot there. Lots of businesses began to question if they even needed to have a physical presence in the markets they're trying to grow—but the answer is yes.

No technology is a substitute for the physical presence you need for relationships and real learning. Zoom is a good way to maintain a relationship, not to build a relationship. It's a good way to maintain communication, not establish communication. It's a great way to avoid having to get on an airplane just to get an update on a project.

But so much is missing. Relationships are built on trust, which in turn relies on respect: and what greater sign of respect for someone is there than actually turning up in person to meet with them, particularly internationally? Or what about the nonverbal elements that make up far more of communication than the actual words we say? Those are in danger of being lost in a remote conversation. In fact, I'd suggest that something gets lost in translation in every communication that is not in person. And then there are those little moments before and after the meeting, the personal time beforehand or the chitchat in the corridor afterward, with the one or two people who were at the meeting who are really interested in what you're talking about. The ability to have those fleeting side meetings creates a more dynamic environment, and that takes people being physically present.

There's only so much you can learn by Googling. I don't know what food in Japan tastes like by Googling it, or what it's like to go to a theme park there. You might say, "That's the way the world is going," but I disagree. At my first business dinner in Japan, someone told me, "Mike, everybody eats and everybody drinks." It's one of the most important observations of my whole career.

When you break bread with somebody and you share a drink, you start to get to know them. You're investing in learning their culture—and the barriers start to break down. It's the same anywhere. Someone comes in from out of town, the first thing somebody says is, "Hey, shall we get a drink or a coffee?" or "Hey, let's go get dinner." We should be celebrating the people who can build those relationships again and again, anywhere in the world. I would often talk about my daughter, Kaitlin, and how she was doing at school. Then someone else would respond with something personal, perhaps about their own kids, and suddenly you're relating on a different level and you're building more trust. The personal investment leads to professional growth.

Team members enjoy a Lohei celebration to mark Chinese New Year in Singapore. Diners toss a raw fish salad into the air with chopsticks: the higher they toss it, the better luck they will have the following year.

MULTIPLE FACETS TO ADAPTING

> The win–win is always when you accept something that's being done locally and you evolve it for them in a way that's brand representative for you.

There are many times when doing business in a different geography will be inconvenient. You might think, we have this sandwich and we're going to sell it to a billion Chinese people, but it won't be like that. They might not want the same sort of bread. Or the filling. Or the packaging is wrong, or the branding, or the pricing. You have to go back to square one. And that is going to be a pain in the butt for everybody.

Disney in California sells millions of churros, which are basically fried bread with sugar on it. If you took them to Japan or China, people would take a bite and say, "That's way too sweet. What is this?" So you need to recreate the formula so that it's not sugar and the bread has a different texture. But if you can get it right, it might be incredibly successful.

I always reminded Disney that Walt Disney himself did not start with a blueprint and say, "This is the only way we can do it." He changed things a hundred times. He talked to people; he got the right financing and sponsors. But when you're a company that has become one of the most respected brands in the world, it's easy to fall into the trap of thinking, "It can't change." Or, if it does change, it's really slow, like turning around an aircraft carrier.

You can speed it up by empowering people on the ground and making them accountable for their decisions. I get that you can't take Mickey and dress him as a punk or put devil horns on him. But you can take Mickey and put him in Chinese costume for Chinese New Year. And you can use QR codes to tell a deeper story, which at the time Disney had never seen. When we wanted to put QR codes on posters in Shanghai because that was what the Chinese expected, Disney folks's reaction was, "We don't even use this technology yet."

Our partners showed us how the QR code could create a deeper relationship with the consumer, and Disney took that lesson and developed even more layers of meaning around the codes to tell stories around the world. With dynamic QR codes, they can keep programming on the back end with different kinds of stories and promotions, deepening consumer awareness and experience even more.

One of the biggest challenges to overcome when you're evolving the way aspects of the business are run, such as technology or marketing or finance, is trying to come to a common ground in different places in the world that still connect to what you're doing. We weren't trying to break completely away from everything Disney was doing. We just needed to take it and evolve it for the way in which business was run in China. The technology the Chinese used helped to create opportunity for both sides. The win–win is always when you accept something that's being done locally and you evolve it for them in a way that's brand representative for you. And then you take that and leverage that across other geographies.

DETERMINING WHAT TO LOCALIZE OR MAINTAIN IS TOUGH

When Pepsi rolls out the red carpet, the carpet is blue, because red is the color of its biggest rival, Coca-Cola. After Pepsi China had given us the blue carpet treatment in Shanghai, I got back in the car with two of my team members. They said, "That was great." I said, "Yeah. And now I've got a big problem."

It was unique that we were even at a Pepsi presentation to provide carbonated beverages in the park. At the time, in any Disney resort or theme park anywhere in the world, you predominantly bought Coke. At the time, Coca-Cola was the Alliance partner for Disney parks globally. That's great for Coke, because everyone wants to be associated with Disney and sell their products inside the parks, and it's great for Disney, because Coke had produced fantastic results. It not only raised a lot of money; it also enhanced the visitor experience because Coke created new products and experiences for Disney's guests to enjoy.

The Chinese were less interested in Disney's deal with Coke

and more in running a fair process that would select the best possible partners for Disney Shanghai, so we had to look for multiple vendors, including Chinese companies in every category, including carbonated beverages.

I started with the president of Coke in China, whom I knew well. I had dinner with him from time to time. Coke welcomed us to their campus, as you'd expect from an existing partner. They gave us competitive pricing of the product and the amount they would pay for the partnership and great ideas to activate that partnership inside the resort. They made a fantastic presentation.

I was also friendly with the president of Pepsi in China through the various trade associations to which I belonged in Shanghai. He said, "We'd love to have an opportunity." I warned him off: "Well, you know Coke is our partner worldwide." He said, "Yeah, I got it. But we'd still love to have an opportunity to talk."

I agreed and visited with a few members of the team to hear Pepsi's pitch. When we pulled up outside the corporate headquarters, there were giant signs reading "Welcome Shanghai Disney Resort" and the blue carpet leading up to the door. In the foyer, there were images of the Disney castle on the walls. There was another picture of the castle on the inside of the elevator doors. When we got to the room, the team told us Disney Shanghai was the account they wanted most, and they started pitching.

They offered great pricing and promised various new developments, including the unique intellectual property they had developed around social listening—judging a business's image from social media users.

It was a holistic package of goods and services that was so competitive for the Shanghai park that when we got back to the car, I told the others, "Now I've got a big problem." I knew I had to make a call I really didn't want to make. It was going to create challenges for us around the world.

I arranged a call with senior Disney executives, including the chairman of parks and resorts, and the Disney CEO. The CEO listened through the whole story and said, "I don't know how you turn that deal down."

Before you knew it, we had a deal with Pepsi. The only one in the world. And that was because the Disney management understood the importance of China and of getting things right for our partners there. Many other companies might have refused; they might have insisted that the global deal came first. Not Disney at that time.

There's a lesson in that story for any company going into China. You'll be faced with decisions that may be counter to what you're doing everywhere else, because there's a very simple truth that every business has to understand if it wants to do well in China. Things that work elsewhere won't necessarily work there.

It's natural in long-term partnerships to get comfortable and just keep doing what you're doing. But when you have the challenge of a new country, a new culture, you have to think differently about the product. Coke can be a really creative company, and they did a phenomenal job for Disney around the world—but in the end it was impossible to ignore Pepsi's commitment and desire to be part of the Shanghai Disney Resort.

We were in a unique position because the Chinese insistence that we try new partners gave us an opportunity to think about what the right partner and the right creative partner and the right financial outcome was going to be for this part of the deal. We reviewed every single relationship we had with vendors who supplied merchandise. In some cases, we did go with Disney's global partners. In others, we chose competitors that had better business models for China.

In the end, the Pepsi deal was a success. Our decision was proven right.

BUILDING EXPERTISE LOCALLY CAN INFORM ADAPTATION

When I worked at Four Seasons, we had hotels and resorts in different countries all over the world. They had standards—the room sizes, the fact you had to have a restaurant, or a bar, or a spa—but the standards evolved a lot. In the beginning, the company used many of the same designers around the world because those designers knew Four Seasons products and standards, they were trustworthy, and the process was efficient and cost-effective. One of the things the company did as we expanded was to start looking for best-in-class designers in Asia, in Europe, in the Middle East, in Southeast Asia, wherever we were building hotels.

We deliberately raised the number of designers because Four Seasons was eager to evolve the product for different cultures, usually using local consultants from big companies with international respect. It helped make the product more culturally relevant in terms of the aesthetics and the feel, but travelers still got the luxury they expected from a high-end personalized luxury hotel.

If someone is traveling from the US to Thailand, they ask themself two questions. First, "Where will I stay that makes me feel safe and gives me the level of service I'm looking for? Some brands come to mind, like Ritz Carlton, Four Seasons, maybe Marriott or Waldorf." And second, "Ah, there's a Four Seasons. Is it just a big brick building that looks exactly like the one in my hometown—or is it cool and different?"

That's what people wanted, just as they did with Disney. They wanted familiarity and convenience, and trust in the quality of the brand, but they also wanted a culturally relevant experience so they could try local food in the restaurants and so on.

Educating consultants and other recruits to your corporate requirements and giving them familiarity on how you do business takes time and money. There's often a concern that the juice wouldn't be worth the squeeze. After you hand them your three-hundred-page standards book, you might get the same thing back you'd get from Joe Blow consultant who you've used for twenty years already. There are two schools of thought. You send Joe Blow over to Thailand to learn, which is how Disney did it with their Walt Disney Imagineers. But that is basically like going on vacation and taking a snapshot of the culture. That's a lot different than when you live someplace. Or you hire someone in the geography who already knows the culture.

I focused on small advances. With a new consultant in the hotel business, you might say, "We're not going to have you design the whole hotel. We're going to have you design the lobby and the restaurant. Then when people see what a great culturally representative restaurant we have, we'll give you the guest rooms in the next hotel we do." As in any business, new contacts need to earn trust with you—and you with them—before their role can expand.

Mike visits a potential site for a new Four Seasons hotel on a headland in southern Japan.

That seems a better approach to me than trying to shove my ideas down the throat of an organization that had been in place for fifty-plus years. The mistake a lot of people make who go international is to want to spin an organization 180 degrees and say, "Nothing you've done works. We will change everything about what we've done and put it in the hands of someone we don't know simply because they live here." There might be nothing wrong with that, but it's far more likely to be effective to make small advances so that people get comfortable and earn each other's trust.

You match cultural representation to the geography because it will translate into better sales. It will make the product or the service you're building relevant to what you're trying to accomplish as a company, which is increasing your market share or building brand loyalty.

Continuing to build trust depends on communication, education, and compromise. It depends on being able to tell the difference between change that is critical to your credibility, which simply has to be done, and change that it is desirable to do. If the latter sort of change is not done today, it's not going to really stop progress or destroy your credibility in the country.

LIVING ABROAD

Living somewhere else gives you a broader perspective on how the world views us and on how you view what's going on at home. You get exposed to a different way of thinking.

Some people, no matter where they are in the world, want to live the same way they live at home, right down to the same brand of ketchup, the same television shows, or the same beer. They aren't willing to expose themselves to new ways to experience life. The other kind of ex-patriate thinks, "Yippee, I'm in a completely different place. I'm going to eat new food and visit local sights. I'm going to evolve as a person, which will be great for me and my family." Those are the people who typically thrive in those environments.

I was in between. I loved being exposed to different cultures, but I was passionate about some hobbies I'd always had. I either had to get up at 3:00 a.m. on a Sunday morning to watch a Notre Dame football game, or I missed it, or I worked deals with my friends and family to tape shows and send videos in the mail. I'd come back from the United States with foods that I missed packed in a suitcase, or medications we couldn't get in China. As you live somewhere longer, though, you start to experiment more, or take local advice, and as you become educated living abroad becomes easier.

Just as companies need to grow and evolve to succeed overseas, so do individuals. It makes things much easier if you embrace that, rather than seeing the job as a sentence you have to serve, like a prison term, before you can go back to your normal life. And in fact, you find that when you do go home, you're not the same. You have a different view on wherever you're from. You have a different perspective on people abroad and you can't slot right back into your previous life. Sometimes it's even difficult to discuss current events with family or friends because you've evolved your thinking.

CULTURAL IMMERSION IS INVALUABLE

By the time my family moved to China, I had spent years living overseas or traveling there extensively for business, and I'd learned how important being part of the community is to helping you understand how to do business there. The biggest lesson Disney learned in the first two decades was about sending in high-powered senior executives for two days a month to try and negotiate a multibillion-dollar deal. They figured out that people have to live there. Their people have to be a part of it. That way they can learn about the culture—and they can educate their business partners about their own culture.

Everything is different when you're overseas, from how you live to how you speak to what you do in your free time to how you work. You have to understand the preferences, the relationships, the tastes, the culture. You have to study before you leap. Just because you were successful in one place doesn't mean you're going to have that same success someplace else. You have to be flexible to evolve and change.

In the United States, the attitude to others is sometimes, "We're right and everybody else is wrong." Living somewhere else gives you a broader perspective on how the world views us and on how you view what's going on at home. You get exposed to a different way of thinking.

My daughter Kaitlin went through middle school and high school with kids from all over the world. That broadened her view and her perspective on culture. It broadened the way she engaged with people who were not from the United States. By living outside the United States, she gained the perspective that the world is a much bigger place than it sometimes seems from inside the United States, with its variety of internal cultures.

She learned that we live at the top of the pyramid. She got to do things like travel that she probably wouldn't have been able to do had she grown up in a normal middle and high school environment. Taking vacations can expose your kids to different parts of the world or different parts of the country, but that doesn't compare to living where they learn to overcome the challenges of melding cultures and getting along with people that have completely different perspectives on what the United States is about and what other cultures are about.

Kaitlin at a restaurant in Japan representative of the exotic ingredients the Crawfords were able to experience by living as expats.

JOINING THE COMMUNITY IS A GREAT RESOURCE FOR LEARNING

Most people find that expatriate communities are warm and embracing because everyone is in the same boat. You share experiences that were different than what you had at home, and you can commiserate or laugh about them. People from different companies feel it's a safe environment to share and learn from one another. I found myself being friends with people that I probably would have never been friends with had I just lived in the United States.

Mike and Kaitlin outside Mike's home in Shanghai, where the homes for the expatriate community were typically oversized: this one had four floors and an elevator.

There are different societies and clubs that help you assimilate and become more aware of how to live and get things done. I spent a while as the vice chairman of the American Business Association of Shanghai because it provided a network that helped educate me on how business was run in China—which helped me make Disney comfortable that we weren't taking any more risks than other big brands.

Everyone was happy to work together rather than compete, but I was lucky. People were particularly happy to help Disney and, later, Four Seasons because they felt that what we were doing was going to make their lives better. People had such a passion about places where they could stay and be entertained that it was an easy sell.

People are always very helpful with the nuances of conducting business as a foreign company in a particular geography you hadn't been in before. There were groups and clubs, and councils were established to share best practices. That's how smart companies learned quickly. Big consultant groups like McKenzie and Deloitte make fortunes by setting up shop in these geographies and imparting pearls of wisdom to their clients, the key pieces of information that will help their business be better. And you can come up the learning curve a lot quicker to be more successful.

After we'd negotiated the deal in Shanghai and were about to start building, we held a presentation for CEOs and presidents of companies that had nothing to do with the resort. We told them what we were going to be doing, but we also set up work sessions to facilitate conversations on specific topics, such as HR or tax collection. It became almost like a convention on how to run a business overseas. Someone from Visa would say, "Hey, is anybody else having this kind of problem?" and maybe someone from Deloitte would say, "Oh yeah, and this is what we had to learn. This is how we do it now." People got in touch with each other to continue talking.

It was always that way, no matter where people came from; everyone was living together in a country that was foreign to them, so they all talked, and shared, and learned.

Mike gives a presentation to other companies and CEOs in Shanghai, updating them on progress to ensure the project had their continued support.

YOUR ROLE IN BRIDGING THE CULTURAL GAP

I built my knowledge about what it was like to do business in China by meeting companies who were already doing it. I'd talk to the local CEO of GM, and he'd say, "I bet you're having this kind of issue back home." I'd say, "How did you deal with that?"

I still remember one of my contacts saying, "If you really want to build advocacy, make your board come here and have a board meeting." That's what we did. We used experience to build advocacy. Once you have experienced something—you've seen it, felt it, tasted it, smelled it—it becomes familiar. It's no longer something to fear and say, "That's different than what we normally do."

The board of Four Seasons was based in Toronto, Canada. My CEO had not been to Asia since he joined the company. They were nice people from a number of countries, but if you told them "This is the culture in Indonesia," you might as well be telling them how Martians drink their tea. I looked for ways to increase their cultural awareness in ways that were easy to digest, rather than trying to force it on them all at once. You look for opportunities to educate through communication, building advocacy, and trust. Sometimes I'd go home to report to them, and other times, I'd bring them out to Asia.

Hotel staff welcome Four Seasons owners to their global meeting, where they learn about industry updates, marketing plans, and new initiatives.

It's my experience that people like to travel and have new experiences. They can take pictures or send their family and colleagues little clips of what they're doing. Even so, it sometimes took a few visits to get a board to understand an opportunity from my point of view. At other times, they understood it at once.

Some people can assimilate things and process them quicker than others.

At some meetings, Disney people would come out thinking it had gone very well, and I'd know that they had bombed. At other times they would walk out saying, "That was painful. Did we even get anything out of that?" And I would say, "Oh, that went great."

Bridging cultural gaps depends on establishing trust through communication, education—and patience on both sides. It's a laborious process. That's why I was put in a position to lead these types of discussions, because I had come up through the Disney ranks. I'd worn a polyester costume. I'd had an hourly worker perspective, a management perspective, and a leadership perspective. I knew what it was to be a frontline cast member, and I'd been at all levels of management, so I could go deep into stories to help the Chinese understand why we needed whatever we were asking for.

I was used to talking to people outside Disney from Singapore, Japan, and Malaysia. I was immersed in the culture, so I knew what Chinese guests would look for if they visited the park. That gives you the perspective of someone on the outside looking in, so you know you have to start with basic education on both sides. You can't just start negotiating on the first day.

In a company like Disney, many people never have an outward-looking role, so they don't understand the interface between the company and the world. From my perspective, Disney has grown dramatically worldwide over the last twenty years, but at the time, it was still used to working with licensees, as they did in Tokyo. Disneyland Resort Paris was the first resort Disney both owned and operated outside the United States. It had learned hard lessons from Paris about what succeeds and what fails, lessons which it had applied in Hong Kong.

Of course, on the other side of the table, the Chinese had their own perception of what had gone well and what had gone wrong, particularly in Hong Kong.

When I wanted to educate Disney, I had to go to other high profile companies with big brands and ask them to tell me about what they'd gone through, because no one in Disney had learned those lessons. I'd ask them, "Would you mind speaking to Disney senior leaders to give them comfort?" I could tell Disney management the same thing somebody from Goodyear could tell them, but it would have far more effect coming from a Goodyear guy who had lived there for ten years. They would say, "That makes sense. I get it. That's good to hear." If I were to tell them the same thing, they'd say, "Hm, are you going a bit local there, Mike?"

BUILDING ADVOCACY

> People like to feel comfortable, so it's helpful if you can bring others to the table that are doing business in the geography already.

While you're working overseas, some of your biggest potential problems come from people at home because of what they know and how they've had success. They worry that you will drink the Kool-Aid and start supporting the Chinese or Japanese or Singaporean way of doing things against your own business. It's your job to gently encourage them to move along on the learning curve. I worked hard to convince people without the same experience or exposure as me to do something different from the legal model, the financial model, the HR model, the marketing and sales model, or whatever.

I would bring in a CMO from another high-profile company to talk to the CMO at Disney, or the head of HR from another high-profile company to talk to corporate HR. Then the Disney person would say, "Okay, they're talking my language. Now I see why you're doing that." I'd invite corporate folks over for a cultural trip, with a comfortable flight and a big car to meet them at the airport. I'd take them to dinner at a fantastic restaurant with a couple of drinks at the bar, and we'd visit the local markets and see some cultural activities. Suddenly it's an experience.

That's the whole Disney philosophy: if you make it more of an event, it's going to have more effect.

Most people don't have the ability to take a step back, relax, and say, "You know, that's a really good point. Let me put some information together. I'll come back to you and we'll talk about that." The natural inclination is to say, "Hey, I'm here and I know this. You have to trust me." That just doesn't work when you're 4,000 miles away and somebody back in California or Florida says, "Hey, Mike, I hear what you're saying about this thing but I don't really believe it because I've been doing it another way for twenty years."

A general counsel is only going to believe another lawyer, trust me. The Disney general counsel took the time to come and meet with a couple of law firms he knew in China, so he gained perspective and understanding. When he got back home, he could say "I've seen this now. I understand it. I talked to a general counsel from another big company. And I buy into it." He became a key advocate.

It was like bringing members of the board of Four Seasons to Asia occasionally to talk to hotel owners there, to look at potential new hotel sites, and to understand cultural nuances in a different way.

The more you can convince business leaders, company executives, board members, or any other stakeholder to come to the particular place where you're building or you're opening a company—so that they can be immersed in the environment and talk to local consultants themselves, not on their home turf but on yours—the easier it is for them to let their walls down and be educated.

People like to feel comfortable, so it's helpful if you can bring others to the table that are doing business in the geography already. Different companies and different leaders are powerful. An accountant would rather hear another accountant tell them, "It's difficult but it's doable" than they would hear it from me. Someone with the same knowledge as theirs can tell them, "I've lived here for ten years. This is how it works. This is how the books have to be done. This is what the government says." That's far more effective than me saying the same thing.

One reservation about advocacy. Don't over-promise or under-deliver. Don't spend your time gaining advocates to help get over an obstacle that doesn't come true—and don't tell your advocates that something is going to be easy if it isn't. You have to be honest. Everyone wants to hear some optimism, which is how you get them to become advocates in the first place. But a dose of reality is always welcome, even if it's difficult for people to hear. Advocates put their reputations on the line for you, so don't go all Pollyanna on them.

CREATE ADVOCACY BY HAVING PEOPLE EXPERIENCE IT FOR THEMSELVES

"We're Disney. They have to understand." If I had a buck for every time I heard that, I'd be a rich man. I had to get allies inside Disney to help convince the company that *no*, the Chinese didn't have to understand.

No one recommends a movie or TV show until they've seen it themselves. No one would advocate for my views without experiencing what I was talking about.

We'd bring Disney people to China and treat them. We'd send them a schedule for the trip, have them picked up at the airport and taken to a lovely little suite in the hotel. In the room, they'd find a nice Shanghai Disney Resort T-shirt and hat, and maybe a bottle of wine and a snack. I'd come the next morning and take them to breakfast and we'd go to a couple of meetings. Then they had lunch with people from Baker McKenzie who are Chinese but speak perfect English because they went to highly reputable schools in the United States and elsewhere. Because the people were credible, the guest felt comfortable as they listened to their stories.

The consultants would say, "You guys are going through a tough time," which is what I'd primed them to say. "Let me tell you what happened to us, and what you need to do to get this deal done." That way the visitor understands that what they are dealing with is not unique to Disney. It's what other big-brand companies have gone through. Now they're not in that boat alone, so they leave that lunch feeling pretty good. I take them out to the site and walk around. They take pictures to send back to their family.

After two days, they are back on the plane. They have had an experience—and they have become one of our biggest advocates.

One word of warning. Don't overwhelm visitors by making everything alien to them. The meals shouldn't all be chicken beaks. You want them to see the familiar too. You want them to feel that this would be a place where they're comfortable to do business. That makes them feel better about what you're doing.

I tried to show visitors a level of respect that was culturally representative of the geography they were visiting. So when they went back to the office, they would feel a little bad if they had to challenge me or say that I'm wrong. I've shown them things other people haven't seen. Sometimes I've had them to my home to meet my wife and daughter, so people become personally invested. That doesn't happen on a Zoom call.

LEVERAGE FAMILIAR EXPERTISE AS NECESSARY

"Abroad" can be scary and disorienting, so fill the geography with as many familiar features as possible. In Shanghai we hired consultants who were best in class but, more importantly, whom Disney had worked with and trusted. Our auditors were Deloitte, our legal firm was Baker McKenzie, our HR consultant was Mercer. These are companies known all over the world. We could have hired local consultants cheaper, but Disney would never accept the credibility of their information.

I also got involved in Western organizations like the American Chamber of Commerce and the Shanghai Committee for Foreign Trade. Any company you could think of was represented: Visa, Pepsi, GM, whoever. Coming from Disney or Four Seasons, I represented experiences that were unique and valued from a personal perspective by leaders of these different companies. I got dozens of business cards from everyone, and I used those contacts to help back up what I was saying to Disney at home.

INITIAL LOCAL HIRES ALSO HELP TO BRIDGE THE GAP

Whenever someone told me, "We gotta hire the human capital to help us do this," I would always correct them: "No, you gotta hire the *right* human capital." You need the right people wherever you are.

We hired a lady from the Communist Party who had been very successful in sales and marketing for the Chinese government. She knew everyone in the government infrastructure. But she had difficulty in acclimating to the Disney environment and the Disney environment had difficulty accommodating her for various reasons, such as the language barrier and how she was used to doing business versus what Disney was used to. There were questions about whether she would be a good fit for the Disney Company. Once you start to peel that onion, however, it always comes down to: "They don't feel good to me because they don't speak my language. They don't know what I do back in the States."

Who are the right people? They are typically a mix of people who know and understand how you have done business or built your product or created your service blended with people that are living in the particular place where you're going to be operating. You don't need all one or all the other. You need cultural carriers who educate people on how your company does what they do in the context of the world. And you need people who say, "Yes, *this* could work, but *this* we need to evolve here because that's not how people in China or people in Singapore or wherever consume what it is that we're doing." Or, "We need to change the fragrance." "We need to change the taste." "We need to evolve the service to be more relevant."

Take McDonalds. In the United States, just about every McDonalds has a drive-through, because we have a culture of being on the go and eating as we drive. In many countries, no McDonalds have drive-throughs, because their culture is to sit down and have a meal and socialize. In fact, that's how McDonalds started, as a place for families who had been working all day to come and enjoy time together. If you force every McDonalds to have a drive-through attached because that's what happens in the States, in many countries no one will use them, so it would be a complete waste of money.

CHAPTER 3

Respect the Culture

Disney has its own culture, and Communist China has its own culture. The deal teams were caught between the two. One of our most important tasks was to find commonalities between the two that would enable us to pull off the deal.

There are two things at play. A company that's trying to develop in any part of the world outside of its home country has the culture of where it comes from. So Disney had a US culture, Four Seasons a bit more of a Canadian culture. But it also has its own company culture, and the interplay between the two sets up lots of different dynamics. When we talk about respecting another culture, you respect both the culture of the place they come from and the corporate culture, the way they do business around a product or a service.

So you have to marry your own multiple cultures with the culture of your counterparts but also with that of the business entity they represent.

Companies overlook that a lot. They either look at the culture of the country that they're going into and forget the culture of the company or entity that they're doing business with, or vice versa. It's a complicated puzzle to solve.

Disney's CEO at the time talked a lot about going into mainland China. He saw it as his legacy. That put us at the forefront of representing Disney culture.

An ideation session on how to bring Disney and Chinese culture together to remain culturally relevant.

STRATEGY

Most companies struggle to implement a strategy for a new market that fails to take account of their own culture.

You can't make deals unless those deals are part of a strategy—and you can't have a strategy unless you are fully involved with your own culture and that of the people you're dealing with.

Your strategy has to align with what makes you successful as an entity—a business or a state or even a country. Where companies get off track is they develop a strategy that they can't execute because it almost goes against who they *are* as an entity. You need to base a strategy around both the culture you're working in now and the culture that you are going to be working in. It's interesting to note that M&A experts increasingly acknowledge that bringing two companies together only works if significant planning goes into incorporating the two cultures into a new culture that everyone can buy into.

UNDERSTAND WHAT THEY VALUE VERSUS WHAT YOU VALUE THE MOST

Many people are wary of China's motives, particularly its approach to IT. The way I see it, the Chinese didn't want to partner with us on Shanghai Disney so they could learn how to run theme parks. They're not out there building hundreds of resorts everywhere. I used to joke to the team that if the Chinese looked at drawings of a ride and stole them, well okay. It wasn't as if it was some secret formula. These weren't nuclear launch codes.

The Chinese wanted to study our IP because they wanted international credibility. That made us guarded, as we knew they had taken IP from other companies in the past. There was a risk—but then, there was also a risk if we didn't go all in on our partnership with the government.

Disney was one of the biggest brands in the Western world, so the deal was an opportunity for the Chinese to show the world, "Hey, we're opening up. We're allowing this kind of business to happen here." They could tell that message to the WTO and to other international trade bodies. They could use it to attract other global businesses, because it gave them reasons to believe they can trust the Chinese.

The Chinese also told us they wanted the deal to help improve the quality of life for the people living there. They wanted to give people things that are fun to do. In the past, the Chinese government hadn't cared about fun, just about finance and trade. Even when we did the deal, many officials couldn't understand why the government would give up farmland to build an amusement park.

At the heart of it all, they wanted good things for their kids. They wanted quality of life. At the time, the Chinese government was collecting brands—and Disney was the ultimate brand to give them credibility in terms of a destination. Having a Disney resort put them very high, because there aren't that many in the world.

It was the same when I was given an opportunity to negotiate a new Disney destination with the Singapore Tourism Bureau. The place was a stopover going from the US to Dubai or from Malaysia to Australia, and the government wanted to make it more of a destination. Singapore felt good to a US-based company. The governing law was British, there was no threat of war and no financial risk. It was one of the financial hubs of Southeast Asia.

The place had a lot of credibility for doing business, which again goes to respecting its culture. It's not about customs, like bowing or going to dinner a certain way. It is about law. It is about financial structure. It is about political or military risk.

Ultimately, Singapore is a small country, and we decided at the time that it couldn't handle multiple theme-park destinations, so Disney pulled out. In the end, Singapore went down another route by introducing casino resorts, but again, what they were after was credibility. The biggest brands can give credibility to a whole nation.

LOOK AT THE HOLISTIC VALUE OF THE OPPORTUNITY

Disney wanted to build a foothold in China to help the Chinese understand what a theme park is and expose them to Disney's storytelling and brand and product. More Chinese were traveling, so they would prioritize going to Disneyland or Disneyland Resort Paris or Tokyo Disney Resort. They would want to say, "I went to Shanghai Disney, but I also went to the other Disneys." That was a big reason to build the park.

It's about the macro impact. Four Seasons was much the same way. Their strategy of building multiple hotels in different geographies was exactly that. If you stayed in one place and you started to learn and understand how the experience was valuable and personal to you, then as you traveled, you had the opportunity to look for and stay in other Four Seasons hotels. You're building brand awareness and creating advocacy for your product and your service. If you do it in each geography in a way that is respectful to the culture, and respectful to their tastes and preferences, then as they travel for leisure or business, they seek out the brands that they know and trust. It may be slightly different, sure, but that's okay. They're outside of their country, so they're already excited about experiencing something that may taste different or look different or whatever the case is... especially if enough about the experience is also familiar.

It's like having a store location on Fifth Avenue in New York City. You may not make any money being there, but you open your brand to millions of people that go to your other stores every single day. Disney knew how many Chinese were expected to travel. We knew what they were spending while they traveled. And we believed that if we created a fantastic product, we'd be able to attract them into our world.

It was a mainly middle-class audience, but just as in the United States, people would save up to come if they possibly could. "I want to be able to take my little emperor, my one grandson or number one child." "I want to be able to say to my friends or to my family, 'I have the ability to do this for my grandson or my daughter or whoever.'" It's like bragging rights, but in a way that has more to do with honor and keeping face within their family or friend network.

The numbers added up. The income qualification was continuing to grow at double digits every year to put people into the middle class. And a two-hour catchment radius from the destination held 300 to 400 million people—higher than the entire US population. We were twenty minutes from one of the world's biggest airports in Shanghai. We had a large mass transit system. All that felt good to us.

REMEMBER THE MACRO IMPACT

Some companies go into China for its own sake and simply want to milk the Chinese. They don't consider the macro impact they can have on mainland Chinese who are leaving China and experiencing the rest of the world. Disney's macro vision was to take the brand to China and expose people to the magic. When they traveled abroad, we would become one of their preferred brands. They'd visit our parks, they'd buy our shirts, they'd watch our movies.

What Disney sells is essentially a version of basic communist ideas about family equality, community affection, and responsibility. In that way, it was more of a symbiosis than a culture clash. The product wasn't threatening. The *Wall Street Journal* published an article that likened Disney Shanghai to a Western aircraft carrier full of Western culture. I squashed that view in one of the very first meetings. I said, "We're not bringing you Western culture. We're bringing you stories of happiness and good versus evil, and immersive worlds that people can live in. Tell me what's Western about that. What's Western about Fantasy Land? What's Western about Tomorrow Land? These are worlds anyone can live in. We'll make them symbolic of Chinese culture."

You can't just make it about a bunch of folks waving the Stars and Bars and saying, "God bless America."

Once the Chinese got to the core of what Disney does, and they saw the kids with the Goofy hats on, and they saw the parents running around with ice creams, they said, "Yes, this is fun. We like this. This is what we want. We want quality."

EXPERIENCE EXISTING PRODUCTS FOR EDUCATION

People in the office back in the United States sometimes had a problem with us looking around China. They thought we were having too much fun and not working enough. My attitude was that if we didn't allow the Chinese government to show us those locations, how could we understand their cultural experience? And how could they trust that we would build the right thing unless we'd seen how Chinese people actually use resorts? You have to spend time going to places, seeing things, doing things, and experiencing the culture.

That was especially true because we could experience the kinds of product we were proposing to build. Social interaction extended far beyond a once-a-month business dinner or having drinks. It was about strategically using social time to build relationships and trust and show them that we were willing to experience similar products to ours to understand them better.

They sent us to a resort named Sanya on Hainan Island, which has many hotels and parks where a lot of Chinese people go on vacation. Then they said, "Okay, you guys have been there. Now, what are you going to do with that experience?"

In corporate environments, there are always questions about expenses. Why did you go to this theme park? What does that have to do with doing a deal in mainland China? Why did you go to this ice festival in Harbin up near Russia? What does that have to do with Shanghai?

It's simple. That expenditure has a direct link to understanding the environment, the product, the service, and the culture, and to building trust.

Individuals and companies sometimes find difficulty doing benchmarking and familiarization tours and trips because companies have to account for expenses. That's true of all companies that I've worked for. There is an eye toward responsible spending and making sure what gets spent adds value to getting a deal done or running a business. That's absolutely an expectation the company should have of their teams or individuals running deals outside of their home turf.

The goal is accountability and education. We wrote reports, we took photos and video, and we leveraged them in updates to boards and line-of-business leaders so that they felt like they were a part of those trips versus feeling envious or left out and questioning the expenditure. But it's a question of accountability. And it's a professional courtesy to ensure that if you are experiencing product rather than sitting in a conference room or a negotiating room, the experience is justified.

The other benefit is that the teams that go on such trips feel more connected to the culture. It gives them opportunities to lift their head up from a negotiating table, take a step back and realize what it is they are trying to negotiate—and the obstacles that may be in their way.

One time, when we were negotiating about the cost of maintenance and upkeep of theme parks, we got a lot of pushback from the Chinese government. They didn't understand why we would put air conditioning in elevators or in lobby areas of hotels, as that wasn't common in China. They didn't see that as a wise use of money. So we traveled around and looked at different parks and hotels that were more akin to what the Chinese government were used to. And we quickly realized that was the experience and knowledge they had. That was what they were basing their negotiation on. Once we were able to educate them on the reasons we needed this stuff, and how it created a different level and added a unique layer to what we were doing, then they understood that the cost was the cost. And we were able to successfully negotiate a higher level of maintenance costs and ongoing upkeep.

A cultural show at the Jade Dragon Snow Mountains in Harbin.

SOCIALIZATION TIME IS ALSO TIME TO EDUCATE PARTNERS

If you're not going to use your social time strategically, you don't need to be in the country. You don't need to be there if you're not going to visit places and you refuse to learn. But any time you *are* there, you're acting as an ambassador for the deal, for your company...and in some cases also for your country. Every time you turn up somewhere, it's another sign that you're taking the whole process seriously.

In return, we took the Chinese on trips to see Disney in Paris, Orlando, California, and Hong Kong. They loved it. In Paris, they'd go shopping for a day and go out to dinner on their own, but we understood that was part of not getting outside of mainland China very often. It was important that they should experience the geographies outside of Disney culture. We invested in allowing them to come so they could see the quality of our product, the investment that went into it, and how we managed it. Then when we were back at the deal table and I brought up, say, a yearly reinvestment for maintenance of the facilities, they understood why it was necessary.

Once we created an opportunity for the Chinese to travel and understand the product in similar parts of the world—in Japan, in Hong Kong, even in Paris, which was different yet similar—they understood that while there were some cultural nuances to doing business in different places, it was really about happiness and family time and date night and other moments of joy that were just as popular in China. That was a key lesson. We got the Chinese to travel and experience the product in other places outside the United States so that they understood we weren't bringing in our culture or trying to impose some underlying belief system that was born out of the United States.

Mike and a Chinese delegation visit the cast of a holiday show at Walt Disney World to experience Disney show production.

The social time wasn't like a formal business trip. We walked around parks and rode rides together. We ate meals together. We had drinks together. We saw shows together. People complained that it was all a big boondoggle. Well, maybe...but it led to building trust and relationships—and that's what ultimately got the deal done.

When I was growing up, my father would always talk about golf being where business got done. That kind of social engagement is a fundamental need. In big companies, that sometimes gets forgotten and everything is boiled down to dollars and cents. It's easy to conclude that the social time isn't worth it—but the key is not to think about it as optional social time. It's crucial education time.

The other side has to understand your product and what it takes to be successful, while you need to evolve your thinking in that particular geography, educate your company, and build the trust that the decisions you make on their behalf—changing a color, a taste, a logo to be more appealing—will work. That education takes time. You don't just walk in and start striking the deal. Just because the senior leader at Disney wanted to make it a focus to go into China didn't mean that every other leader of particular lines of business within the organization understood that and was completely aligned. They were still nervous and unsure about how they could support to help make that successful. There were still a lot of obstacles to overcome, although it helped that the CEO had laid out the vision.

When you have to get buy off internally, it takes time and education and going back to the right consultants, the right peers in the market, the right organizations. That's how you prevent leaders in your business from feeling they're the only ones who are exposed. It's all about education.

MUTUAL VALUES

I believe that giving teams the freedom to align those values and marry the cultures is what's allowed for success in the deals I've had a part of and the teams I've led.

People in the West have a shallow view of doing business in China and East Asia, full of caricatures they've picked up from TV. Everyone knows some of the rules. It's true they might seem superficial, but they're important, like always shaking hands with everybody in the room or remembering to present your business card with two hands. That's stuff anyone working there should just know, but there's also a deeper level. If you have a dinner or meeting between two senior leaders on either side, you exchange scripts so each side knows what the other is going to say. That way, nobody gets embarrassed. You ask what gift they're giving to your senior leader so that you know what gift to give theirs so that the value of the gifts are fairly equal. Again, it's about avoiding embarrassment. When you're putting placement cards out for a table, think about who sits next to one another, so no one more senior is sitting beside somebody too junior. Buy the right level of gifts so there's something for everybody, but they can't be the same. They have to be of different levels. That's the level of cultural understanding and appreciation you need when you're in somebody else's house—which is where you are.

What's more important, however, is seeing where you can align your product or service and what you represent to appeal to the community you're moving into and the new consumers you're serving. That makes negotiating deals and getting work done a lot easier.

You have to keep your team very well coordinated. You always have to look for the wins for both sides and maintain a professional, coordinated approach to leading your negotiating team so that everybody is informed. You need to remain focused on the bigger picture, always, not arguing over something that may cost you something even more important, which is your mutual values. I always talked about no surprises. Even when you're trying to resolve conflict, it's crucial to make sure that each side understands the purpose and goals. Exchanging the scripts was an example of that. It made sure there were no surprises so that both sides could prepare for each other and be respectful of one another.

It didn't mean you couldn't go off script, or you couldn't have an opinion about what was being said as the conversations evolved, but having at least a baseline understanding was important. Some of that back-channeling communication really helped align goals and made leaders feel comfortable in a position where they could come together and negotiate out final agreements.

The Chinese believe you're in their house. When they come to your house, they'll do things differently, the way you usually do them. But when you're in their house, you have to do things their way.

YOU'RE STILL DEALING WITH INDIVIDUALS

It's not like you sometimes hear. The people across the table are individuals like you. They're operating in a different system, true, but their motivations are similar: looking after their family, professional advancement, personal satisfaction, a legacy, and so on. They're as eager to succeed as you are: and they might suffer more if they fail.

If my deal team didn't get the deal done for Disney or we did a deal that was okay but not great, there was *no* real risk to us in any way, shape, or form. Maybe we wouldn't get a promotion anytime soon, but that was the worst that could happen. On the other side of the table, there was always an edge. If something didn't go the way the government wanted it to go and someone was responsible for that, it wasn't clear how those individuals would be handled after the fact. Their careers could potentially stall out. In the communist system, there are differences in the ability to accept a different outcome versus the ability to accept it from a Western point of view. There has to be evolution in thinking to deal with these differences, so much so that there were times that I had to remind the companies I worked for that it was okay to force those differences to the forefront. At times we had to stand our ground, but we also had to understand that when we did that, we had to then give them something in return so that they could save face. That way, the other side of the table could continue to be empowered.

And that was the goal. When you're dealing with other entities, success ultimately depends on how empowered the individuals on the other side of the table are and how much they can do to help support the final goal.

On many occasions we gave the Chinese air cover because they had something they wanted to present to their ranking government officials but they didn't want to get criticized for it. They'd say, "You guys can present this and be the bad guys." That was fine by us, though we never asked them to present to Disney. When I felt we had a stalemate, I'd arrange for the CEO to meet with the mayor or the party secretary to talk through it.

BRING A PRODUCT WHERE EVERYONE CAN BE HAPPY TOGETHER

A ride is a ride. It spins, or it goes up and down or sideways. The difference between Disney and a traditional thrill-ride park is that Disney themes its rides, usually based on a universal story or premise that might come from a movie or from real life. When you go on the Pirates of the Caribbean boat ride, you're inside a 3D representation of the movie.

That was Walt Disney's genius. He wanted to create a world where people could go and actually immerse themselves in the environment. They would check reality at the entrance and be welcomed into a world of fantasy and adventure and excitement.

It's the same today. When you walk through the tunnel and come out in the park, your cell phone doesn't matter as much any more. It's just something to take pictures with. You get on the Small World ride or the Lion King ride or the Star Wars ride and you enter a whole world.

That's why the rides are expensive to build. We took multiple familiarization trips to other Disney parks so that the Chinese could see the detailed storytelling that goes on in developing the rides. Normal rides can cost a few million dollars, but for Disney it can be well over $100 million. But that's why they charge over $100 per person per day to visit the resort.

One of the biggest complaints about Disney Hong Kong was it had nothing new. Visitors said, "I've been on this before." For China, we realized we needed new rides with completely different and enhanced technology. We created a brand new Tron Cycle rollercoaster, based on a remake of the original Disney Tron movie, based on real high-tech technology. The ride didn't exist anywhere else; even the story didn't exist anywhere else. The Chinese loved the blend of brand new things. People want to see things they know presented in a completely different way.

At Four Seasons, the founder and leadership team had one golden rule (*the* Golden Rule): that they treated others as they wanted to be treated. As they went into different parts of the world, they had to learn *how* people wanted to be treated. In both cases, it's a question of the business understanding that their team was doing things in a way that was representative of treating people as they wanted to be treated. When they were designing hotels or theme parks or whatever else, they had to make sure the environments were immersive for the culture and familiar to it, but also that the brand was still acknowledged as being unique and different from other companies.

That's the lesson for every company. You have a product, you have a service, you have something that makes you special. It's how you align your values that will really create the secret sauce and give people the opportunity to be a part of it. That was what I always tried to do. I believe that giving teams the freedom to align those values and marry the cultures is what allowed for success in the deals I've been a part of and the teams I've led.

CULTURAL LESSONS ARE MUCH DEEPER THAN SIMPLE ETIQUETTE RULES

You have to go beyond the rules of etiquette to respect the people and their background. This was particularly pronounced in China because they weren't used to anybody telling them the truth. In the 1990s, they had grown used to Westerners coming in like prospectors in the Gold Rush. A lot of companies saw China as a place to get rich. "We'll put our product there, we'll do as little as we possibly can, and we'll make a whole bunch of money because there are a billion people there."

That eroded trust from the Chinese toward Westerners. That sometimes comes as a surprise because in the West, we see it the other way around. We think they're the ones who can't be trusted.

That's how they negotiated, too. They constantly tried to re-baseline you to something so low that anything they got near that was a win for them. It took me a while to educate them that that was not going to work with me. I wasn't trying to manipulate them to win a bunch of things and put them in a difficult position with their bosses in the government. It wasn't my style. I had to figure out, "Is this real? Do these guys really think they can do a deal with these kinds of terms?"

I went to consultants and peers in other companies who told me, "Look, you're just getting the same kind of treatment that Westerners gave them for the longest time. You have to earn their trust before you're going to be able to negotiate on real terms."

It's a question of education on both sides.

CHAPTER 4

The Art of Negotiation

When you set out on a complex negotiation, it can be difficult for people back home to even imagine that it will ever be done. My attitude was always to keep the ultimate destination in mind but only to concentrate on the next step. When we were negotiating in Shanghai, the senior Disney executives really started to embrace the view that this was how difficult deals were done. We did enough and we kept it going, but achieving success was a bit like Donald Trump's winning the presidency in 2016. No one believed we had a chance, but then we'd do enough to survive the next step, and then the next one. There comes a time when everyone involved, and those watching back home, understand just how complex these deals are. And there comes another time when they look back at all the steps you've taken, and how far you've come, and think, "Holy heck! We're going to get there." It reminds me of a senior Disney leader who once told me about the Shanghai deal, "I didn't think this was ever going to be real. And now it's almost done."

OBJECTIVES

> Once you have alignment on ultimate goals and timelines, you can break tasks down into objectives and ensure you have the right people.

Any deal you make has to fit your goals as a company and how you want to build the company according to your vision and mission, but the people on the other side of the table often have different motivations. When I negotiated with Cirque du Soleil in Tokyo, for example, it was simply an expansion of their product. They already had a show called La Nouba at Disney in Florida, so we were discussing the extension of that relationship. When I negotiated with the Singapore government, on the other hand, their aims were completely different. They wanted to become a more international destination where people would stay longer, and they were looking for credible assets to help them achieve that.

ALIGN YOUR OBJECTIVES

At the start of negotiations, agree with the other side on "What are we trying to do here?" Once you're aligned on that, the next question is "What is your timeline for that?" Once you're aligned on those two basics, you start to break the deal down into subcategories. What are your key business issues? What are your key legal issues? What are your key governance issues? That's when you start adding the heads of those particular teams to bring expertise to support discussion on the key milestones and topics.

At this stage, expertise and experience are less about helping you generate a to-do list of items to check off and more about creating a roadmap of things to consider and pitfalls to watch out for.

Everyone has some view on how their company wants to operate, but it's worth remembering Mark Twain's old adage: "It ain't what you don't know that gets you into trouble. It's what you know for sure that just ain't so." A lot of companies or individuals get themselves into trouble because they walk into a negotiation saying, "I know exactly how this should work because it's worked before and by God, it's going to work the same way here as well." The key for me was having individuals who were curious about the differences between markets while also reassuring the company that they had consistency of approach.

My success was always based on using our experience and learnings from elsewhere to develop our own roadmap and a custom checklist, not simply using someone else's checklist from a different negotiation in a different geography.

SUBSTANCE OVER FORM

In China, you can't own land. And certainly not in perpetuity. Instead they gave us two consecutive fifty-year terms. Such restrictions can be difficult for big brands such as Disney because they appear to introduce an element of unnecessary risk, which understandably is something that businesses try to avoid. And yet the laws in a communist country like mainland China can very rarely be changed for foreign companies. The reality is that even when you've had success in asking governments or partners to do things one way in other places, it won't necessarily work to ask them to do things the same way in different places. The laws are different, the culture's different, the partners are different.

Risk makes people nervous, but it's important to remain realistic. I heard that a senior executive in Disney had allayed concerns about the land deal by saying, "Look, tomorrow the Chinese could roll tanks right down the middle of Main Street. And there's nothing we can do about it. Don't create a false sense of security around a long-term deal lease. It wouldn't matter. They could just turn up one day and say, 'Sorry, we don't do this anymore.'"

The thinking was that doing that to the Walt Disney Company would risk making the Chinese government look really bad. That would make other companies stop and think, "Do I really want to go over there and do business? If they could do that to Disney, they're surely going to do it to us. If they're really going to take advantage of one of the biggest-profile companies in the world and kick them out, we'd better think twice about what we're doing here."

Imagine the headlines: "China Catches Mickey in a Mouse Trap" or just "China Kills the Mouse."

WINNING DOESN'T MEAN THAT SOMEONE LOSES

You soon judge what progress can be made by whether the other party brings the properly ranked individual to the table. For me in Shanghai, that was the local Deputy Secretary of the Communist Party, Chairman Fan. In the due diligence process, the process goes from your selling them on what they could do as a part of the experience you're creating to their selling you on how excited they are and what they're planning on doing. That's when you know that you've got them. They want to be part of whatever it is that you're proposing.

The individuals matter. Chairman Fan headed up Shanghai

Shendi (Group) Co., Ltd., the state-owned company created to partner with Disney. He was used to people just saying yes whenever he spoke. He had never really negotiated international deals on this scale before. That made it incredibly challenging. I can't even call it arrogance. The culture of communism and the Party had simply conditioned him to understand that everybody else would fall in line with his point of view.

I had to find a way to help him understand what we needed without him losing face. There was a lot of back-channel communication. It slowed things down, but it allowed him to buy into the process and meant I didn't have to say, "Hey, it's this way or no way." It was a slower but more deliberate message that helped him shift from, "You're telling me something different from my idea" to "I like what you're saying and I have this idea about how it could work here."

Success means that both sides win or, on occasion, that both sides lose and are equally unhappy. To create a stronger partnership that can last for a long time, you need to minimize the perception of loss and create a new way of thinking for both sides. It's not about losing something to get something. It's about evolving our thinking and changing the perception of what a loss actually means. You're giving to get.

Any issue has to be a problem for both sides, not just one. I've seen companies treat issues as if they're only problems for the other side. It might be more of an issue for one side or the other, but in the final analysis, both sides have to resolve it with neither feeling that they have lost. That's something I preach all the time: winning doesn't mean that someone loses.

BEING AUTHENTIC WINS TRUST

When I go around the world, I take Ohio with me. It fits me very well, and it's a superpower. It's enabled me to do lots of things. I'm a pretty plain-spoken guy who does what I say I'm going to do. If I'm not gonna do it, I say no. You take me as you find me; I take you as I find you.

That's the way to make deals. There is no art of the deal. There's no shouting or bullying or playing tricks. Speak plainly and assume other people are reasonable until you find out that they're not. Some people don't always say what they mean and mean what they say. They put on shows or get confused about what's important and what isn't. They don't make deals that succeed.

Going to Asia was a big transition for me. Arriving in Japan was like being a child all over again, learning how to walk, how to read, how to talk. But to be honest, moving from Ohio to Florida was almost as big a change.

My hometown of Willard, Ohio, is small-town America. It's in the heart of the country, where the Industrial Revolution took shape with railroads and industry and farming. At one time, Cleveland, Ohio, was the richest city in the world. The Rockefellers lived there. Today, it's seen as having a slower pace of life and lacking sophistication. The people are salt of the earth, and a lot of them wouldn't contemplate leaving Ohio. When I was growing up, I never envisaged myself going around the world.

The young Michael Crawford.

That small-town outlook shaped my career. People ask me, "Are you a Midwesterner?" I say "Yeah, I'm from Ohio." "Yeah, we can tell." Early on, I thought nothing of it, but later in life, when I'd lived outside of Ohio for longer than I'd lived in Ohio, I started to say, "How can you tell that?" The answer was pretty consistent. People could see a genuineness, a humbleness, a you-get-what-you-see mentality that they appreciate. That helps when you're doing deals or structuring a business opportunity. It builds trust that I'm not a swift-talking guy from New York or LA.

My father always told me, "You're only as good as your last at-bat." I truly believe that all the great things I've been a part of in my career don't really matter for what I'm doing right now. They gave me experience I could draw from, but if I'm not successful as President and CEO of Hall of Fame Resort & Entertainment Company, that's the only one people will remember. It's sad, but it's true. That's why I always focus on the next steps forward. What I've done in my past doesn't interest the community I'm in now, or the shareholders who have invested in my company, or what my daughter thinks of her dad's efforts today.

You're only as good as what you're doing now. No one gets to live off what they've done in the past.

Coming from Ohio, I always felt like I had to earn everything that was given to me. I never felt entitled to anything, and I never felt like I was smarter than anyone else in the room. I listened a lot. I offered my opinion when I was asked, but I was humble about it. That allowed people to be more open, more direct, more trusting of me.

It's not an act—it's just who I am. It's served me well over the course of my career.

It's hard to play a slick-talking game when the other person at the table is open and direct and ready to take chances. If people try to negotiate by throwing out an outlandish demand, I just say, "This is what I'm willing to accept. This is all I can give. If you come back and say you want more, my answer's going to be, 'That's all I can give.' And you know that it's true." That kind of style brings the slick talkers and the people who see themselves as high-end negotiators down to a level that is more helpful to getting the thing done. I get them to feel good rather than feel that they have to outmaneuver me.

There's a saying in football that teams play down to their competition. You can be a really great team, but if you're playing a team that's not as good sometimes you let your foot off the gas and play at their level. That's how it is in business, too. I'm not the dumbest guy in the room, but I'm not the smartest guy either. That creates an opportunity for those who are smarter to be more authentic in what they're talking about.

IDENTIFY BIG PILLARS YOU WON'T COMPROMISE AND ITEMS YOU CAN

The Chinese mandated that in every category of partnership we would go out and look at many different suppliers, including at least one Chinese company. We had a list of hundreds of pieces of merchandising, from T-shirts to rain jackets and umbrellas to plush Mickeys to pins. We went through it line by line to discuss where we were sourcing it from. A good percentage was already sourced in mainland China, but the Chinese wanted us to source 100 percent from mainland China. They built in the idea that the wider Chinese economy had to benefit from the Shanghai deal.

We showed them how some of our deals were better for them. Our umbrellas all came from a country that produced all the umbrellas for every Disney park around the world. The economies of scale made it a win–win, because we involved the Chinese in the bigger Disney deal, which ultimately saved their investors money. Maybe one day all of Disney's umbrellas will be made in China, but for now that was the best deal for both sides.

In the end, you might have to make some decisions in the interest of your partners that seem counter to your company's way of doing things, but if it's going to be moving you in the right direction, then it's a case of giving to get. In the future, you'll still arrive at where you want to go.

Companies have to consider their really big pillars, the intellectual property or business they want to protect, and make them clear up front. And they have to accept that everything else can be negotiated. If it matters more to one side or another where your umbrellas are produced, treat it as a test case to see how business has to be different in particular parts of the process.

PARTNERS NEED TO FEEL THAT THEY ARE A PRIORITY

We got the idea from the Chinese that their general impression of the Disney park and resort in Hong Kong was that it was too small. They were also concerned that it used existing attractions from other places around the world, predominantly Disneyland in California. The mainland Chinese government said, "We want something new and unique. We want you to be creative for us and think about Chinese culture. We want different and new rides and shows. You can still tell the same stories, but you have to tell them differently."

For your new partners, you're only as good as the last thing you did. They compare what you've done before with what you're proposing now. If you're proposing to replicate the same product or the same service that you're doing everywhere else, it might save you time and money, but it can also lead to resentment with your future partner if it makes them feel like they're just another business deal. If you come to the table and say, "This is the way we always do it and you have to accept it," they'll feel that you're remaking an old business deal. You have to treat it like a brand new deal.

The concern in China was that the "magic of Disney" would just give them the same old things that Disney did in other places. They looked at Hong Kong Disney, Tokyo Disney Resort, and Disneyland Resort Paris for things they were concerned about so that they could avoid the same mistakes. Their attitude was: "We don't want to be embarrassed by what we do. We want to be able to boast that Shanghai Disney Resort is incredible; it's got unique rides and shows and new technology, and it's very respectful of Chinese culture."

That was a tall order.

The large-scale model of Shanghai Disneyland used for education and display with the Chinese government and other public partners in Shanghai.

You can't go into China on the cheap or in a substandard way because of its sense of national pride. It's a country that wants to grow in profile on the international stage and be seen as a world leader. They're not interested in second or third place. They want to be at the top.

One of the reasons to bring key individuals into the negotiation process is to show the other side that they are your priority. This isn't just another deal to you; it's something important. You need to make them feel honored that you're bringing in leading subject-matter experts to support you. And of course, you have to avoid having the experts come in and just repeat the same old song, chapter and verse, about what you've done before, which will only deepen suspicion.

At Four Seasons, I had a business development team that did virtually all of the negotiation, but I still went to the meetings to help start the deals. I wanted the other side to understand that the deal was valuable to me as a senior leader and to understand that while the team on the ground was fully empowered, I was also there if they needed me. The people on the other side of the table need to know that you care enough to be there, to share your views, and to listen to theirs. Bringing in senior leaders gives you credibility and makes the other side feel more valued.

HELP BOTH SIDES SAVE FACE

The financial investment in Shanghai was reported to be the largest single investment Disney ever made in a theme park outside of the United States. But it was absolutely necessary because it unlocked so many things. Four or five major issues, such as creative control and management control, were all predicated on the investment.

Disney placed a high priority on building its brand in mainland China, as did Four Seasons. The key for both companies was how to show their commitment in a way that made the potential partners understand that the companies were serious and willing to take risks on things like land investment, lack of market sophistication around understanding the product, or the other things that big branded companies face when going into developing markets that haven't had the level of product or service they're producing—and that might not be ready for them.

Companies that make decisions in new markets every day know that the key is balancing risk with commitment to your partners. It's like the stock market. Not every investment makes significant returns, but if you play the long game, eventually things grow and mature. Your partners have to feel that you don't have an approach where you are just there for a quick buck. They have to believe that you won't just pull out if you don't reach profitability within a year.

For the Chinese, it was less about money and more about face. They wouldn't give us stuff if we were not willing to invest alongside them. Why would we give you the control if you have no risk? They already knew we were sharing the brand risk because I made it clear that if this failed for the Disney brand, that was significant for us as a company, but they wanted us to share the financial risk, too. When I convinced the Disney leadership to agree, I went back and said, "I have agreement on a significant investment amount. Now I need these two or three other things." That's how I moved the roadblocks.

BRIDGING DIFFERENCES

> The key for me was having individuals who were curious about the differences between markets while also reassuring the company that they had consistency of approach.

If you want to be successful in different parts of the world, you have to identify cultural differences and figure out the best way to marry what you're trying to achieve through your product or your service with what the other culture needs and what it uses in its everyday life.

It's key that you find out first where the cultural differences are and how what you're trying to accomplish aligns with the goals of the other party. It's the same no matter where you are in the world. You need to understand the other side of the table. Then you can try to tailor an experience or a product to what they want.

When you're negotiating a deal, you first have to understand where the differences are before you can bridge them. Some will be cultural. Some will be business differences. Some will be alignment around costs or goals around revenue. But some will be truly fundamental.

Those things are important to get on the table early so that you can quickly discern whether or not you can actually do a deal. I've learned over the years that if those differences are actually too big, it may not be possible or worth the effort. You might have to make a judgment call earlier on or be so transparent with the other side that you say, "Look, you have to understand we're not even close in terms of aligning. The difference may be too great to overcome. Do you still want to continue?" People respect you more for being a bit more direct rather than wasting time for what could be weeks or months or even years.

A young Kaitlin Crawford models clothes in advertisements in Japan, where her looks made her visually distinctive and glamorous.

Companies sometimes think, "We're going to take the same formula of peanut butter that works great in the UK and put it in Malaysia." They do that for three reasons. Number one, it's a lot cheaper than introducing changes. Number two, they get a false sense of security around something that's already been successful. "If it tastes good here, it'll taste good there." I call it the *Field of Dreams* approach: "If you build it, they will come." Number three, they forget cultural nuance.

Every culture has something unique. I learned that in Japan. The Japanese see themselves as being different. "We don't like the same food as China. We don't wear the same clothes as Americans. We don't treat our kids the same way as Singaporeans." That taught me to evolve my thinking because it showed me there were many ways to be successful using the same brand and the same philosophical approach to deliver great experiences, immersive worlds, and environments. You can do it in a way that represents where you are, rather than simply lifting from elsewhere.

We once showed a marketing campaign that had run in Hong Kong to the mainland Chinese. It was very effective and touching, so we thought it would be really impactful. Their first comment was, "Those people are Hong Kong people. They're not mainland Chinese people." You can't just switch cultures in and out. Customers want to see themselves in the product. They want to experience it in a way that's relevant to them.

Disney's traditional philosophy was to send out the best subject-matter experts, operators, and designers from the United States to different locations because they would know how to do Disney better than local talent. Disney's approach is to measure every movement and make sure that the spatial planning and the layout align. Nothing is subjective. Everything is metrics. Industrial engineers must map out everything: the space for the rides, the number of parking spots, the distance from the rail station to the front gate, everything.

I didn't know if that would work in Japan. I'd already seen the difference along Main Street, where we hold the daily parade. The Japanese all sit down to watch the parade on their tatami mats—so you need far more space along the edge of the avenue than in the United States, where everyone stands up.

Cultural differences can impact the way metrics are accounted for. That's the same for any country. The work ethic of certain employees in Europe may be different than in Asia or in the Middle East. The same holds true with cultural or societal norms. People may be used to having much less personal space in certain areas in Asia versus the United States, where people like to have more room. In Japan, the laying out of mats to be more respectful was one of those cultural norms where traditional metrics would fail, if you were looking at your business through the lens of what has worked in almost every other place around the world. Observing and being educated to understand that these were the differences we were going to face allowed the parade route to be bigger, so there was more space for those mats to be laid out, to be respectful of the Japanese culture.

I always made sure folks visiting from the US were paired up with people who had a different perspective; they had figured out the geography and knew where we could compromise and what we couldn't. If you're stubbornly company-centric, you'll fail.

That didn't prevent us having a difficult conversation when we had to tell the Chinese that their creative talent was not quite sophisticated enough yet to do the work. We had to bring in a lot of Japanese ride developers and engineers. There's a specific discipline called artistic painting, for example, which is painting a wall to look as if it's really old and cracked. That skill didn't even exist in mainland China. We had to employ hundreds of artistic painters from different parts of the world to work alongside Chinese artists to teach them.

That's an important lesson. You're in this for the long haul, so you can't simply bring in a bunch of experts to do the work. Once they leave, there's no one to do the work on an ongoing basis. If you don't have local service providers, like artistic painters or ride engineers, you're going to be paying a fortune to fly people from around the world to come and help.

Our philosophy was to mandate the contractors to work with the Chinese and educate them, because we knew we were going to be building more rides and other hotels and theme parks. We wanted to do it locally to keep the cost down—and it was also an easy way to keep the mainland Chinese happy.

The option is to bring an American worker over into a geography where they don't know the regulatory environment or the development laws. If you develop the local group, they can develop relationships with the building departments and the inspectors because they share the same culture and language. They can get things done a lot more efficiently than foreigners do coming back over and over again.

Companies that are good at this, like Starbucks or McDonalds, find international development executives who know what to watch out for every place they go. They never start from scratch. They have a playbook that says "We've done this, so now we can do this." They have the confidence of their company, too, because they know how to do deals that are relevant for the geography but also for the mothership. They find a way to acclimate what they do in their product or their service to be culturally relevant.

Some companies that are successful bring in "task-force teams" to help educate the local team or the local contractors or whoever is building or producing the service or product. The team is temporary; it eventually leaves and they hand the reins over to a local team to then run the business from that point. They don't leave a bunch of expatriates that cost a fortune in whatever market they're in.

They bring people in, they do the training, and as they're training, they're also learning and helping their subject-matter experts in the product or the service. They're good at doing these things in different markets. They are watching out for it in their mind, so if the local team is telling them "That may be too sweet" or "That may be too bitter," they can quickly evolve their product and training differently.

There are business development executives who do these kinds of deals all over the world. Four Seasons has business development leaders in Europe, in the Middle East and Africa, in Asia, in the Americas. Those individuals do multiple deals, so they get much better at it and are more efficient.

LEARN THE STRUCTURAL FRAMEWORK

Every culture has its own structural framework for business, and you need to understand it. If you don't like it, you'll need to make a strong argument for an alternative. In Shanghai, the mainland Chinese wanted the governing law on the deal to be mainland China law. Disney insisted on Hong Kong or Singapore law, which is essentially British law, so it's trustworthy and not open to corruption. That fight went on for a long time. We learned from other companies and then showed the Chinese how other folks had done it, not just for ourselves but also to help our Chinese counterparts, because they didn't know everything either. We would tell them, "Look, you allowed this company to be governed out of Hong Kong. Why wouldn't we be allowed to be governed out of Hong Kong?" Then they'd take that knowledge to their bosses.

On an ongoing basis, we had to figure out everything we were doing—the enforceability of the control over IP, the name, the rights to operate the park—in a way that could work for Disney. We had to stretch, but so did the Chinese, because they had to give us the right controls for us to be comfortable. It got to a place where both sides needed each other if it was going to work. There was no chance that either side was going to give everything.

We constantly had team meetings so we could understand the most important things each particular negotiating team was hearing and where we could develop a strategy to trade the horses so that we got whatever was the biggest thing we wanted.

Banking was one concession. We wanted to bank offshore, but the Chinese wouldn't allow it because the government had gotten burned by companies doing that in the 1990s. That caused problems because we'd have to take documents down to the local tax authority to send to the provincial tax authority. Our people sat there all day waiting for the authorities to stamp the documents so we could access the money.

The concern was that we'd make money, but it would be stuck in China. Ultimately, we got comfortable with that idea because we decided that if it didn't come back to the States, we would use it there. Our natural hedge was to use it for growth and other business in mainland China. So that became a concession to get other things we wanted.

The land deal was another concession. Chinese law would not allow a company or anyone else to own land. Disney had to settle for successive land-lease deals with fifty-year options attached that were automatically renewed. Nobody had ever tested the renewal system because, at the time, China hadn't been open for fifty years, so that was another leap of faith.

In fifty years, would they have the right to kick us off the land? Maybe. But at least we had documents to make a legal challenge. More importantly, we had the court of public opinion, which is important to the Chinese in terms of face and reputation. We'd be able to say, "We had a deal, but now they're reneging on it." So we agreed to make the successive deals, as long as they were all signed up front, as if they were simultaneous deals.

And we took the leap of faith.

Backhoes on site at Shanghai Disney Resort.

There are common lessons for anyone managing for any company in a similar culture. When it came to hiring, for example, we had to consider title growth along with pay and other nuances to benefits and plug the new approach into the systems we were used to. That needed a lot of work in benchmarking and hiring consultants. Meanwhile, leadership had to build the bridge with our own company and their traditional thoughts around marketing or HR or finance. That doesn't happen simply by you telling them what you need to do. It happens by bringing in other subject-matter experts and benchmarking off other companies.

THINKING STEPS AHEAD

If you're trying to win, you're not going to set us up for long-term success. Don't feel that compromising on something means you're losing. In order for us to win, they don't have to lose, or vice versa.

When you're sitting in a meeting, you have to think three moves ahead, because that's what the people on the other side of the table are doing. That's what the Chinese government officials are doing. That's what your bosses and counterparts back home are doing. It's a mistake many companies make. They just deal with what's in front of them, without thinking about the precedent it will set or the impact it might have on future decisions. If you're not thinking ahead, you're always reacting and you'll always come off as being really defensive when you're put on the spot.

I always told the team, "We're playing chess, not checkers."

LOOK OUT FOR THE DOMINOES OF DECISIONS

I'm reluctant to make simplistic observations, but it seems to me from having negotiated in Asia that people from Western cultures often find it easier to give way on points rather than fighting over them. That's particularly true of isolated situations that can be solved by making a compromise. You might think, "Who cares? We can give them that"—but that's not a negotiating strategy. A negotiating strategy would tell you that if you give on this one thing, you should be prepared, because that one thing is attached to that other thing, which is attached to that one, and then to that one. What seems like an easy, isolated compromise might be the first of a whole series of dominoes that you don't even realize are there.

Understanding that would sometimes put me in the position of arguing against my own company. The company might be inclined to agree to something, but I'd tell them to say no. That way they could give me cover to negotiate a better position.

You can sometimes see a pattern emerging when you're doing

business in China or in other parts of the world. People will ask you to move ten miles farther than they need to go and then be happy when you agree to move one mile.

They will try to re-baseline you. That's another reason to be diligent about negotiating in good faith. It will allow you the opportunity to call someone's bluff in a meaningful way.

I don't condone anyone losing their cool in any negotiation, but there are times when you have to walk away. You should walk away professionally, but the other side has to see how committed you are to doing things with high integrity, so both sides honor their word. If your partner isn't doing that, they need to see that it will create problems. Walking away is sometimes necessary to do that.

There was only one occasion when I walked out of a meeting. It was just a day or two before a big national holiday, and the Chinese had around thirty senior leaders in the room. They came to the meeting and changed something we had agreed on. We had a deal two days before, which we had spent a painful week negotiating, and all of a sudden the story was completely different. I said, "This is bad faith. If this is how you're going to negotiate, there's nothing more for us to talk about." My counterpart on the other side said, "Hold on, hold on. Let's talk about it." I said, "There's nothing to talk about if this is really the way you guys are going to negotiate. We've negotiated in good faith. We didn't change anything, but now I have to go back and be embarrassed in front of my senior leaders."

I said, "As far as I'm concerned, this negotiation is over. You guys can think about it more—I'm happy to give you time—but there's no reason for us to be here." I stood up, packed my stuff, and proceeded to walk out. The team watched me and didn't know what to do. None of them moved until I turned around and said, "That means all of you too. Let's go."

As we were walking out the door, someone on my team whispered to me, "Are you going to say anything about enjoying their upcoming National Day holiday?" And I said, "Screw it."

If you're not willing to walk away at times, the other side won't give you respect.

Thankfully, when I called Burbank afterward to say, "I think I just blew this thing up," they said, "You did the right thing."

That time, the Chinese backed down, but they continued to try the same thing, albeit less often. They'd say, "I didn't think we had agreement on that." I'd say, "My notes show that this is what you said." They'd say, "No, we didn't say that," and we'd show them the notes. I made everyone take notes in every meeting so we could come out and compare them.

I still have all my notebooks.

I'm not sure if what we learned is still there in Disney. I guess they'll find out when they try to do another big park somewhere in a different culture.

DON'T TELL THE OTHER SIDE WHAT TO DO; ASK THEM FOR HELP

After problems with the capital structure of Disneyland Resort Paris, Disney wanted the Chinese deal to have no commercial debt. No banks. Everything came from equity and shareholder loans. That caused months of discussion because the Chinese could not believe Disney would not use other people's money. It was a meaningful change compared to how they had done business before, but as Disney made publicly clear, it was to ensure that the company had final control over its own destiny. I had to explain to the Chinese why it would be a bad look if something went wrong—say a global health pandemic—that forced us to default on their payments to the banks.

The Chinese did not want to get embarrassed, which is what happened in Paris, so that decided it for them. They understood that we weren't going to shut the lights off in our own park, and neither were they.

These were unprecedented differences in business for them, but it wasn't one-sided, so they didn't feel cheated. Both sides had things they didn't like, but both sides got the things they needed. I remember conversations with my counterparts when I said, "I'm going to tell you right now, there are three things on this page I can give up. There's two that I can't. I need your help." I never told them that they had to accept anything. I always asked them for help.

That was a different style than they were used to. One of them said, "Mike, you just say things very truthfully and very directly. That's much more believable than trying to put on a big show." I told him, "I don't know how to do it any differently. That's just my style. I'm just a Midwestern guy. I'm not trying to beat you. I'm just trying to explain what I think we need to do to be successful."

People can tell authenticity from maneuvering to do a deal. Instead of negotiating by saying, "Can't you just go 50–50 with me on this," it enables you to say, "On this one, I need you to give me the whole point that I have here, but on the other one I can do what you need for you." There are times where you have to have certain points. In those cases, be very open and honest with them about the reasons why. On the other hand, there will be times in Asia where you may not understand why they have to have a win. In those cases, keep asking the questions to get at the *why* behind their insistence. That allows you to deal directly with the issue you're trying to resolve. It doesn't mean you can or can't accommodate them. Your ask just means there needs to **be a good reason for the request.**

IF YOU DON'T ASK THE QUESTIONS, YOU DON'T GET THE ANSWERS

On some negotiation issues you sometimes think, "I really can't believe we're wasting our time on something as trivial as this." Perhaps we didn't understand why the Chinese were insisting on it, but it's the same whether you're negotiating with a communist government or with your partner. You need to try to understand what's driving the issue rather than trying to win an argument. You have to be like a litigation attorney in a courtroom. You keep asking questions to get to the answer. The witness won't just tell you. You have to keep going at it to understand.

Companies that are successful are authentic and genuine in their reasoning. They have supporting information. They show the why and take the time to explain it, versus just saying, "This is important to us and we have to have it." Once you understand, it's easier to look for a compromise that can meet both needs. But if you go into the negotiation with just one position you have to have to be successful, you won't ever get anything done, especially in the face of lower level resistance.

Your counterparts aren't going to simply tell you why they are having an issue with a proposal. You have to ask a series of questions to find out. You get to a place where you can say, "So that's your problem with this particular issue? Well, that's not a problem. I can handle that. I can do XYZ. If you can give me this, which is *my* biggest point of focus, I can make that work."

The Chinese government and our partner organization, Shanghai Shendi (Group) Co., Ltd., were very focused on developing the area around where Disney was building the resort. We said, "Hold on a minute. Why are you developing assets five blocks away that are going to potentially compete with the assets that we're investing in together?"

They wanted to build a hotel right next to the resort. We said, "No, you can't do that. We're building two hotels together. If you build a hotel and it's cheaper, we're going to lose money." That wasn't their issue. They said, "We're giving up all of this farm land and we can't just let it sit empty. We have to show the land is being used." We said, "You have to let it sit empty because it is future land for the growth of the resort."

The discussion went back and forth for days, but it became clear that the government in Beijing wasn't going to allow them to take farmland and let it sit empty with no promise of development. So the deal team tried to get us to commit to timing for other developments. And we said, "We have to wait and see if the park is successful or not, and how much land and what we need to develop."

Ultimately, however, because we understood what was driving their issues, we got to a place where we worked together. We worked on a project on the periphery of the park to make sure that it would at least complement what we were doing rather than compete with it. That was the compromise.

Disney's first response was, "No way are we going to allow them to do this. This is our property. They can't do that." Well, for one thing, it was not *really* our property. In addition, the Chinese had looked around the world and had seen that every single Disney resort had other hotel properties built around it. Every single Disney resort had shopping and dining and other entertainment properties built around it, feeding on the overflow. The Chinese sold their government on the idea that this was how they would protect the land. It was also a way for them to generate some revenue on their own to make Shanghai Shendi creditworthy. They were a shell corporation, but like any other company, they had to show that they could generate revenue.

We couldn't stop it, so the compromise was to make sure it was done in a way that was noncompetitive and complementary. With our input, they built some small hotels mainly to host government officials, but the hotels weren't themed and had different price points than the hotels in the resort.

On the one hand, we acquiesced once we understood their needs.

On the other, they had to understand our points around non-competition and the best chance for success. I told them, "If you build stuff and it outperforms our hotels, that's going to bring very negative press for the resort and for China."

GET COMFORTABLE WITH A SLOW PACE

The deal behind Shanghai Disney Resort took decades. Many individuals and teams worked to lay the foundations and break down the barriers. My phase of the negotiation came relatively late in the day, after the corruption scandal in the Shanghai government had shut down negotiations for a few years. The Chinese wrote Disney saying, "Okay, we're ready to reengage now." The head of business development at the time had seen me lead multiple deals almost to completion. I told him, "I want an opportunity here. I don't want to be the business lead. I want to be the lead on the entire deal negotiation. I think I can do it the way I know from Japan and those other deals. And that's with a team that goes and stays there and builds relationships, not a team that flies in on Tuesday and leaves on Friday."

We thought that doing it that way would cost more because of sending a team to live there, but also that we could get it done in six months. Four months later, we were at a meeting in Shanghai and I said to the team, "Remember that six months? That's not going to happen."

Things move at a slow pace, depending on your deal partner and their objectives. Westerners want to get in, make decisions, and get out. In other cultures, they want to study and understand. They pass decisions up the chain and back down. You need the patience of a saint because you talk about the same thing seven different times without a decision. Ultimately, there will be a trigger that makes it happen, and sometimes you'll understand what it is and sometimes you won't have a clue.

In all, it took Disney twenty-five years to do the deal, but if they had done deals early on or even toward the end of that time, they would have had a horrible outcome. They would have rushed and made bad decisions. And in the end, the outcome wouldn't have been anywhere close to what we achieved. Although we took a new approach in getting our team on the ground, the fact was that both sides were finally ready to do the deal. If both parties aren't ready, it doesn't matter who you send or how hard you push—the deal isn't going to get done.

When you head to the deal table, you have to have a sense that both sides are ready. Then you can look for the win–win. I've started many deals for companies that have the deal they wanted already set up in their minds. The challenge with having a predetermined outcome related to specific deal terms means you have to win on all of them or you're going to lose. That only makes losing more likely. It's far more effective to walk in saying, "I don't have any specifics in mind as to how this has to be done."

You can have a roadmap to provide guardrails of things you need to be successful. We knew we had to have a certain amount of land to build a Disney resort or a specific location for a luxury hotel, for example. But the more specific your predetermined outcome is, the more it creates a mentality that anything that differs from that outcome represents a loss, and anything that matches it is a win.

That's not a recipe for a good partnership, in business or in life.

No one gets up with a predetermined path for every single step they'll take throughout the day.

Toward the end of negotiations, we started having all day and all night sessions. That was when we finally set a deadline for the deal, when we agreed after two years that the big pieces were all in place. We set a groundbreaking ceremony for Bob Iger and the Shanghai mayor and the Communist Party secretary. When the Chinese agreed, I knew they would get it done because there was no way they were going to be embarrassed by failing.

That was when we saw them start to make decisions in the room.

By then, we had narrowed down the list of items to resolve from hundreds to tens, and the Chinese gave their deal team more latitude. As long as they didn't get outside of the primary deal parameters, whatever they came back with was good, so they started saying in the meetings, "We're okay with that." There were many sessions toward the end when we'd start at 7:00 a.m. and go until 2:00 a.m. We'd take four or five hours to sleep, then come back and do the whole thing again.

LOOK FOR THE WIN-WIN

Sometimes the hardest things for people to do become the easiest things once they understand why they are doing them. It boils down to whether people are willing to set aside their egos to do something that can really work for both sides. I told the team many times, "If you're trying to win, you're not going to set us up for long-term success. Don't feel that compromising on something means you're losing. In order for us to win, they don't have to lose, or vice versa."

A late night negotiating session in Shanghai as team members and interpreters work on the final deal points for Shanghai Disney Resort.

I heard some stories that senior executives at Disney doubted that the Shanghai deal would ever get done, but most could see that it wouldn't be done if Disney insisted on having everything done its own way. We focused on ensuring the key objectives we needed for long-term success were still intact. We concentrated on what was critical for the company to be successful, and that's how we convinced the Chinese that we wanted them to be successful, too, as our partners.

We didn't resolve every issue in a predetermined manner. It's like hiking through a forest. No one insists on sticking to a single path if there's a lake or a boulder or a bear in the way. You find a different way to the same destination, but you don't have to take the exact steps you thought you would take.

Most of what I've learned has been through taking something

that has been successful as a high-profile brand and recreating that success in different geographies. It involves marrying a culture with a product or service, which requires understanding and education on many different levels.

I've done it successfully with two very high-profile brands with an approach that was consistent for both. I dealt a lot with leadership; cultural acclimation; a willingness to understand compromise and accept it as a win, not a loss; and an understanding of the kinds of talent you have to surround yourself with.

THE PEOPLE YOU'RE DEALING WITH ARE LIKE YOU

Once you know the rules of engagement, it's easier to build trust. Sometimes the Chinese would come back with something that wasn't the same as when we had discussed it, but we learned that was just how they worked. It didn't mean they were trying to cheat us.

We always felt some of the Chinese team had been picked because they spoke English better than they let on, which was probably a strategic advantage for them. They had perhaps been educated in the West or had dealt with Western companies in China, so they were generally quite open and worldly.

Outside of their role as government officials, they were very likable and caring. When you walked into a government building in the middle of winter, it was rare that the heat was on, and the buildings were like giant mausoleums. I remember one Saturday morning negotiating session in the early days when it was colder inside than it was outside. We brought light jackets because we had come from a warm hotel in a warm car and we assumed we were going to be in a warm building. They noticed we were cold, and as we broke for lunch, a lady walked in with some clothes they had purchased for us because they could see our lips were blue. We thought that was a remarkable gesture of goodwill.

I realized then that we were dealing with people like ourselves, and I was thankful. They had been given a really difficult task, to bring in this big Western cultural behemoth without it embarrassing them, but the Chinese side was very excited about dealing with us, just as our team was excited about helping build Disney's presence in mainland China and allowing people to experience a new and exciting themed destination that was unlike anything they'd seen before. For us, the deal was a big career opportunity. Some of them confided that it was for them, too. If they could get this done and strike a fair and balanced deal, they would climb the ladder quicker.

PIECES CAN FIT IN DIFFERENT PLACES IN THE PUZZLE

With a small team stuck in the middle of two great monolithic cultures, the Shanghai deal was negotiation in its purest form. We were negotiating both ways, toward the Chinese and back toward Disney. At that level of negotiation, there are always pieces that can fit in different places in the puzzle—even though the puzzle ultimately has to show the picture you want it to show.

The Chinese always reserved the right to go back and change their perspective on something. They argued that this was because they hadn't had the entirety of what it was they were agreeing to in front of them all at the same time. They'd say, "Conceptually we know what you're saying, and we can accept that, but we have to also get to a place on these next three items where we understand fully your perspective on those."

In the West, people are used to the idea that once you've agreed to something, you've agreed to it. It can be difficult to understand why that wouldn't be the case in China. But before the Chinese had the full picture of things, they didn't want to lock themselves into anything. It was often problematic knowing what was actually agreed and what was simply a holding agreement, like a stepping stone to unlock the next few points.

I didn't always operate as the Chinese were used to. I would walk in and say "We talked about these three things. We agree to them." They would look at me and say, "Hold on, are you agreeing right now?" They couldn't believe we didn't want to talk about them again. I was the other way. When you have a log jam, you have to shake a log loose. I was well over my skis but I had to measure the risk I took with my response. When you're at the table, the other side must feel that you have complete authority. That way, they can trust the comments you make.

There were times I told a white lie and said we had agreement when we didn't, simply because otherwise I couldn't get Disney to move on the next two or three items. There were times when I was well over my skis in sand. I didn't want to get sucked into a situation with someone saying "Okay, let's go back over this thing you say they've agreed on." When that happened, I had to go back and play the same trick as the Chinese. I'd say, "Now that we've seen the next couple of things, we no longer agree on this one exactly the way we talked about it."

Circumstances pulled the rug out from under me a few times, but only enough for me to wobble, not enough for me to fall down and bang my head. I'd say to their deal team, "If you do this, you're going to cause me to lose face with Disney. And if I lose face with Disney, the trust could be gone. And then I can't be sure we'll still be able to make things happen the way we have been making them happen."

They understood that, because everything was based on the trust we'd built up between the deal teams.

Key to that trust is the strength and confidence of the senior leader. It empowers the people that are negotiating the specific deal points by giving them decision-making autonomy. Senior leaders who are insecure and have to make all of the decisions ultimately will not have success. They will make their team very nervous to do deals. No one will go out on a limb in terms of trying to be creative if they feel that the senior leader is not confident in the individuals' abilities.

Whatever you're negotiating now, you're also looking a number of steps ahead because if this doesn't happen, that can't happen, and then that can't happen. It's a high-stakes game, and if you get yourself sucked into concentrating only on the next move, you're going to lose.

You have to deal with whatever is coming your way right now, but you can also keep an eye toward the end goal and how today fits into that. And the next three days, and the next three months. I relied on process mapping, and the timelines and alignment it provided were really important.

You have to look down the road, which is why we identified quickly those long tentpole items that were critical to us: access to the land, creative control, ultimate management. You have to decide what they are and get them set up, because otherwise you can't start putting up all of the smaller poles that give you stability. My tactic was very simple. I always assumed I had the authority to agree to things until somebody told me I didn't. I was happy sometimes to say that we had agreement in order to lock in the Chinese by saying, "We have agreement on our side; you have to get agreement on your side. If you can't, then we can't move forward." They didn't like that sort of pressure. They sometimes had to go all the way up to the politburo to get things approved. And we had to recognize that they were playing for high stakes in their careers.

ADJUST YOUR WAY OF THINKING

The Chinese are masters at asking for the entire world when all they need is a tiny piece of it. They understood that people from a Western background feel bad when we can't get agreement on something, so we at least start looking for a compromise. The Chinese, on the other hand, can say the same thing for days and weeks and months, and not feel bad about it at all. They have no emotion about that.

Many times I told companies that I worked for, "Don't feel bad. You want to be nice, but if we give them something every time they ask, they'll just ask for more. It becomes a learned behavior, like when you give a child candy to stop them complaining so they just complain more." Once they know that if they ask for something far out you'll give them something even close to that, that's how they negotiate. It's very simple, but in Western culture it makes us feel bad and creates anxiety.

I'd tell my bosses, "Just say, 'No, that doesn't work for us.' If you give any inkling of even considering a proposal, to the Chinese that means we're going to agree to something very close to what they want. And then they just dig in and stay in that position."

That was a huge cultural lesson for everyone. There are times when you have to be very calm and very clear because leaving any ambiguity will cause misunderstandings and delays. If you don't say no, the Chinese take it as meaning yes. Give them an inch and they take a mile. Every single time. I had to almost fight my own company to get them to understand that if they gave in to this, this is what they'd be asked for next. We think we're compromising to build trust, but that's not how the Chinese see it. They perceive that you're giving in to their request. It's a test... and you just failed. The next test will be even more egregious, and you're going to feel bad and progressively feel worse and worse. And you'll end up with a bad deal.

It was useful to understand what Disney would agree to, if all else failed. But there were many times I held back their agreement and simply said, "We can't do that. We can do something significantly less that's still going to help." I was protecting the company from itself because I was living it every single day. Like anything else, unless you're living it, you can't fully grasp the cultural differences you feel in the room.

CHALLENGES

> When you have an upfront commitment, I always start with, "What are you trying to achieve by doing this deal?"

Confidence is essential—but maintaining it is a huge challenge. On at least a few occasions I came pretty close to overstepping my authority because I didn't want to be seen floundering, either by the team or by the other side of the table. The people you're negotiating with have to be confident that you have the authority to say whatever you're saying. If they spend time and energy negotiating points and you come back and say, "I couldn't get that approved," they wonder, "Why am I talking to you? Get the person here who's empowered to make these decisions."

The launch point for big deals usually starts with the senior-most people coming together and saying, "See that person there? They're empowered on behalf of our company to get this deal done. They'll keep us informed and let you know our positions. If we come to a stalemate, we might have to come back together and help them, but until that point, I need to know that your guys are also empowered to make decisions." Otherwise everyone is just spinning their wheels.

Negotiation tends to be circular. We had working teams that talked about particular challenges and brainstormed potential solutions. They'd come to me for guidance and support as to what they were proposing, and I'd raise those points with my counterpart. That way we kept an aligned view.

Asian countries often seem to have quite regimented approval chains. In China, Japan, Malaysia, and Singapore, you had to accept that no matter how big a title the person on the other side of the table had, they had to go back to their superiors more than I would to mine. It helped for us to surface our key areas of focus as efficiently as possible so they could work the waters further up the food chain. You have to help them avoid a situation where their bosses tell them, "Sorry, we didn't tell you that that was okay. You can't do that deal."

My team was made up of executives who were subject-matter experts. They were people I trusted who had been involved in deals or had lived overseas or a combination of both. They were good at what they did. Things only got kicked upstairs to me when they couldn't come up with answers. It was up to me to figure out the compromise opportunity, if there was one, or where we would take a harder line on something or give on something else.

It took years to sign the deal, and then the physical elements— the rides and the shows—were fixed because those take a long time to build. We tweaked a few things with newer technology or newer cameras over the four- or five-year build. That's what the operating team was learning about—how we sold merchandise and food and beverages or how we avoided black-market ticket sales by tying tickets to government-issued ID cards. That was brand new for Disney, even after doing Hong Kong Disney and Disneyland Resort Paris.

Mike signs the deal at the official project signing ceremony.

THERE'S NOTHING THAT CAN'T BE OVERCOME

There's always a deal to be done if both sides want it and they're both empowered and willing. It may happen more slowly because you have to take the time for education and getting people comfortable, but there's nothing that can't be overcome. People would say, "I don't know how you do this." I'd tell them, "It's amazing what you can get used to." The threshold for pain grows the more pain you have endured.

When you have an upfront commitment, I always start with, "What are you trying to achieve by doing this deal?" That answer will tell you from the start whether they're sincere about needing this for some reason that is important to them or not. You need to walk away from those initial conversations believing that they are committed, that they've dedicated resources and put financing against it, and that it's a strategic priority for them. The same for your own company. You need to know it's a priority and get a commitment up front.

For Shanghai Disney, that commitment was given right off the bat by Bob Iger himself.

NEGOTIATION IS NOT A POWER PLAY

It's your job to help the team recover from mistakes, because mistakes will happen. Make them believe in themselves even when they fail. The Chinese often undo stuff that's already been done, but I don't like backtracking and saying, "Listen, we need to go back over it again." If you do that too often, you start to lose trust and you open the door for them to backtrack too. So I would always try to cover any mistake in future decisions.

"Because we gave you X, we now need Y." That way, if you fumble the ball once in a while, it's not going to cost you the whole game.

Negotiation is not a power play. It's a marriage where each partner tells the other what they need out of it. Hopefully those things align and allow them to stay together, because the point in getting married is not to get divorced. If you go into a deal without being sure that this is who you want to be your partner, that's a problem.

It was my job to tell the Chinese what we needed to be successful long term and to convey it in a way that made them understand that I was also considering their side, too. "I've got something that you want—this product, this brand, or whatever—and you need to be able to trust that when I finally get it here I'm going to operate in a way I think will allow me to be the most successful in your particular geography. Why would I take on the risk of failing? I don't want to fail for my company, for the brand, for the customers, for the investors."

You both make concessions to show your commitment, and you build trust until you get each other to a place where neither of you can unravel what you've done. It's like once you get married and you have a joint bank account, a shared house, shared names, shared credit cards. It's very difficult to unravel, unless the relationship has gone to a place where neither side any longer shares the same aligned vision of the future.

Once a deal is done, you can't have one side feeling every day that they got screwed. If that's the case, divorce is coming. A good deal can withstand the test of time because it has a strong foundation and both sides trust each other. You can't come out of it thinking, "Wow, did I fool these guys!"

PLAN FOR FAILURE, BUT DON'T EXPECT IT

No one can see into the future, so you have to build in as much protection as you can in case things don't work out. I've spent far more time negotiating what happens when the partnership doesn't work than what happens if everything is going great. Dispute resolution mechanisms take forever to agree upon but ultimately are necessary for both sides to know there is a way to resolve issues professionally. If the parties' interests are no longer aligned, you have to have discussed the way to achieve an acceptable outcome.

It's not fun contemplating failure. It's completely counterintuitive to the positive thinking you usually need during negotiations. But it is necessary so that both parties trust that the other side will honor requests and needs if they do disagree and that there's a mechanism for doing it.

STAYING CONNECTED

When you're the boots on the ground overseas, you have to keep folks at home in the loop.

When you're facing the other team across the table, you've got your back to your own side—but they're still watching you. When you're the boots on the ground overseas, you have to keep folks at home in the loop. People in Disney started thinking, "There's something going on over there but we don't really know what it is. Is this deal going to get done? How's it going to impact us? How's it going to impact *me*?"

Being inclusive is critical. I'd go back to the States once a month to provide an update on progress and to make sure everyone was in sync. I encountered a lot of nervousness about what commitments we'd made that couldn't be changed. People worried that we'd given away the family silver. We hadn't, but it was a constant reminder of the need to keep reassuring the Disney board, other Disney senior leaders, and executive line of business leaders that we hadn't gone too far. When people don't know what's going on, they substitute their version of the truth for the real story—and that only causes them worry.

You need to maintain relationships with the mothership, or you'll be perceived as "going rogue." People may be concerned that what you're doing is going to set precedent or jeopardize the way they run their own lines of business. I spent a lot of time going back to my headquarters to have one-on-ones with people in charge of business units to explain things to them and get their perspective. Getting consensus is just as critical on your own side as it is with your counterpart. You have to listen to people's concerns, you have to make sure you're trying to consider points of view from within your own company, just as much as those of your counterpart.

This is something companies forget. They empower their international teams to go do things, but those teams sometimes forget the bigger picture. I knew what I was doing had to be completely different from what the rest of the Walt Disney Company or the Four Seasons group was doing, otherwise we weren't going to be successful. So I helped to evolve the companies' thinking around what made them successful so they would be successful in these other geographies.

Mike with Jack Ma, discussing business opportunities in Ma's office as president of Four Seasons Portfolio Management; they stand in front of an early Picasso Ma bought because someone commented that they thought it looked like him.

You can help your company understand how other companies have done business wherever you're at by bringing in key subject-matter experts in HR, finance, legal, and so on to provide air cover. Deals are done before the final handshake, so you have to make them understand that you're looking after everybody's best interests, not just one particular line of business. If you have to give on something to do with legal, you can balance it by getting concession in another area, such as marketing. Winning as a whole is far more important than winning as individual lines of business or individual units.

GETTING CONSENSUS WITH YOUR OWN COMPANY

Disney didn't say no to many things; instead they said, "Help us understand how what you're proposing to do differently won't dilute the brand." That required nuances and involvement. I welcomed executives to mainland China and showed them other companies. We hired local communication experts for public affairs and marketing from high-profile companies so they could help educate the folks from Burbank as well. We had to get them to understand that the macro was about exposing our brand and the stories and the quality to a population that was going to influence the rest of the world for many decades to come.

I told the marketing and brand teams, "You need to start thinking about putting Chinese television stations into Walt Disney World Resort in Florida and in Disneyland Resort Paris, and Chinese language magazines, and Chinese-speaking front desk hosts and Chinese-speaking interpreters. The wave is coming and you want to be up on the surfboard."

We were influencing culture inside the company around the world, just as much as we were bringing culture into mainland China.

CHAPTER 5

On the Ground

It felt to me as if my career had positioned me well to make the deal in Shanghai, after living in Japan and being involved in a lot of travel and international deals. My operational experience, business experience, international experience, and business development background all put me in a strong position. That made it hard for the Chinese team to argue with me about operating a park. They would often say, "It's different in China." I'd say, "How so? Do the Chinese *like* to wait in lines? Do the Chinese not eat food? Do the Chinese not want to buy merchandise?" Those things might vary a little, but fundamentally it's still the same business everywhere.

That was very impactful to my counterparts. They told me, "Look, we've grown to trust you because you're direct. You might not tell us good things all the time, but you tell us the truth. We know you've lived in these worlds and we know you have a good understanding of them."

It was the same at Four Seasons. The company had grown very successfully under its original management, but management wanted to develop a new business strategy, originally for Asia, because that was where a third of the company's growth was going to come from, but ultimately in a much larger region. I was there to think broadly about how to grow their brand in both the residential business and the hotel business.

The view of Shanghai and the Oriental Pearl TV Tower from the penthouse of the Four Seasons hotel in Shanghai/Pudong.

It was the company's philosophy of high-level service that had made it successful, but management was interested in seeing what someone with a more diverse business background might be able to contribute. I could help because I knew how to use my personal experience as an expat to gain credibility professionally. If I lived in a place and experienced social settings or visited hotels or theme parks, I could then talk more credibly to my counterparts at the deal table.

When I originally took the Disney job in Tokyo, it was a gamble... and an intimidating one. But it gave me a chance to learn a lot about being an expat and working with different cultures.

Wherever you are and whomever you are working for, being an expat is particularly challenging because you need to maintain the balance between personal life and professional commitment. Everything you do has an impact on your family. One key for me was that my wife was committed to being in Japan, and later in China, because we saw it as an opportunity and experience to learn about new cultures. We also let my young daughter Kaitlin have her own input on the move. When you make decisions as a family, you have a lot more successes than you have failures.

LEADERSHIP

A big part of the role for any leader leading a team or helping grow a brand overseas is to provide air cover.

Too many senior leaders are trapped by their own egos. People seriously say things to you like, "My CEO won't do that. They have to be the first one to walk out on the stage. They have to be the first one to speak on the podium." Ego is what kills most deals and most business relationships.

That was something I appreciated about my CEO at Disney. He was great at what he did, but he didn't have an ego about it. If there were twelve of us staying in a hotel and we were meeting at 7:00 a.m., he was the first one down at 6:50 a.m. Nobody had to wait around for him. He wasn't the last person on the bus or the first person to speak. He created a symbiotic relationship where everybody felt appreciated and valued. That made it so much easier for me and the team.

There's an excitement to being able to give your company a new presence in a place it's never been before or to grow it where it's been small. That's why Disney was so excited about moving into mainland China. It wasn't just a technological advance. It wasn't just another fifty new movies. It was making an impact on an entire civilization, which is a rare opportunity—and I was fortunate to be able to do that multiple times.

Big international deals, and sometimes domestic deals, are a long haul. Your job as a leader is to find the right team and give them clear direction—plus whatever air cover they need. And you need to keep them motivated by celebrating the key milestones on the way, so that they can see the next mile and then the next rather than getting distracted by the length of the marathon.

When we went to Shanghai, I told the team I thought it would take six months. It turned out to take two very intense years.

We survived by taking multiple small steps, celebrating the

achievements, and ensuring everyone knew their place in doing something historic for such an iconic company. We had the motivation of visits from leadership, and we made sure the team got the support and the credit.

The leader models the right behavior. There are always potholes in the road to getting a deal done, so I always tried to model patience and positivity, and I always tried to ensure that everyone felt equally appreciated. There's always a way through the challenges, both in your own company and with your deal partners.

One key is to communicate even the smallest points, because it's inclusive and it helps people understand the why behind the decisions that you're making. The *why* is critical. You're not telling them, "This is what we have to do." You're saying, "This is *why* we have to do it." Once people understand the why, there's a greater likelihood of getting to a better answer than if you just say, "This is the way we have to do it."

LEVERAGE EXPERIENCE FROM WORKING WITH OTHERS

When I was at Walt Disney World Resort from 1995 to 1999, I was asked to be a part of a business development team transforming an existing property that included two locations side-by-side, a nightclub district called Pleasure Island and a shopping and dining area named the Village Marketplace. Disney owned and operated every single restaurant, merchandise shop, and entertainment experience in both, but the feedback was that guests were leaving the property because they had had enough Disney. They wanted to go eat at other restaurants or have other entertainment or shopping experiences.

Disney didn't want them to leave the property, and I was brought in to play a small part on the deal team because I was an operator who was used to working with outside brands, like Cirque du Soleil, Virgin, and Wolfgang Puck. When we brought "outside" brands onto a Disney property, we had to make them understand that they were part of an integrated, immersive experience, not a standalone outlet. Disney wanted me to help educate both the business development team and the companies they were talking to, so over a couple of years I changed from being a pure operational person to become an operating and business development person.

I was the person who said, "Hey, House of Blues, if you're going to come here, you can't have acts that are going to be spitting blood on guests. You have to understand the environment that you're in."

After being a small part of deals, I was able to grow from that and continue to gain a reputation as someone who could be trusted to negotiate on behalf of a Fortune 500 company, or another massive brand like Four Seasons. Being overseas, working with the Japanese, and learning how to negotiate operational strategy, marketing strategy, and continued brand oversight in that environment allowed me to be somebody who understood the balance of relationships and building trust. That helped me become the lead of a negotiating team and part of a negotiating group for the Walt Disney Company that extended the brand in multiple different geographies around the world.

It was great to learn negotiation as the face of an international giant. Most of the firms I dealt with had half of Disney's brand profile. That gave me a heck of an advantage.

Some partners are easier than others. I worked with a fast-food operator whose people were particularly arrogant to deal with. In one meeting, we spoke about volume and how many people would come through a destination we were creating called Downtown Disney. We told them, "You have to remember that at Disney, you have tens of thousands of people who are very focused on getting food quickly throughout the day. They want to get back out to have their experiences. You might need more stations and points of sale." They pushed away from the table with a smirk. Their attitude was, "Look guys, we're a huge global company. We know what volume is. We understand how to deal with lots of people."

On the first or second day of operating the property, their regional vice president (who hadn't been in the negotiations) said, "Wow, we've never seen anything like this. This is the busiest we've ever seen an outlet. This is unbelievable volume."

That kind of experience in dealing with third-party venues at one of our properties supported my role in Japan. The guy who interviewed me said, "You really don't know a whole lot about our theme parks, but the experience you have in managing relationships, in helping create experiences that are different than Disney yet are integrated into what Disney needs, is invaluable for us, as is your ability to negotiate with high-profile brands that can be pretty arrogant. The credibility that you bring from that perspective will really help us with our Japanese counterparts and the relationships that we have there."

In Japan, someone else owned the destination. Disney had a license agreement with them, so we were there to oversee how they operated it and how they leveraged the brand. I had to learn how to manage the experience through others, and that gave me a lot of confidence that as a deal partner I could help people see their own role and the role of my team and of the company. It only underlined my belief that to be successful in a place like Asia, or anywhere in the world, you have to be able to achieve success with other companies supporting or even delivering the mission that you set out.

There will always be partners who get pieces of the pie. There might be partners who get the whole pie.

It doesn't always feel great, but it's inevitable. Get used to it.

A team research trip to Tokyo Disney Resort.

TAKE TIME TO RECOGNIZE YOUR TEAM

The senior leaders at Disney were great at personal relationships. The CEO would come over to Shanghai at least twice a year, maybe three times, which was a lot for someone so senior.

Once when he came, the team had been grinding every day for two or three months straight, with no weekends. He was going to have lunch with everyone. I told them, "Remember, you don't often get a chance to sit in a room and have an informal lunch with a CEO of a company like Disney. Be honest, but be professional. Remember you still have your careers." Everyone was a bit cranky, so I reminded them, "He will remember if you are rude or negative."

When the CEO and I had breakfast that morning, he said, "How can I help? What would really help when I meet with the team?" I said, "It would mean a lot if you told them, 'I know what you've been going through.' They've had three months of nonstop grind and there are times it feels like we're making no progress, but we are. You could reassure them about that."

He listened and delivered it perfectly at lunch. And he said, "What can I do to help make your lives easier?" Without missing a beat, one of the key members of the team said, "I really just want to be home for Christmas. Do you think we can do that?" The CEO grinned and said, "I think we can make that happen." He told me, "I don't care what's going on. Make sure the entire team is home for Christmas and New Year's."

My team member asked me later, "Am I fired? I'm so sorry. It felt natural when he asked what he could do." I said, "Why are you sorry? You were honest. You were professional." She said, "It felt kind of petty." I said, "It's not petty to say that you'd like to be with your family for a holiday like Christmas when you've been working your butt off for this long."

The CEO understood that you have to play the long game in

a big deal. If you lose the team, it can take a long time to get them back.

MAKE SURE EVERYONE GETS THE MEMO

One of the questions the team asked the CEO at our lunch was, "Can you help us create more awareness with people back in California?" He asked what they meant. "Well, sometimes we get challenged on things that the company doesn't understand." Someone even told him, "You're here more than most other people are here."

I've been in that environment a few times in my career. The CEO and the top management want something to happen, but then there's a disconnect. The next layer of people don't quite understand what the heck is going on. There's always someone who hasn't got the memo.

An invisible bubble separates the people sitting at the top from everyone underneath. The people underneath fight like heck for the things they know have been successful, and the policy and the procedures that are already in place. They don't like change. A big part of the role for any leader leading a team or helping grow a brand overseas is to provide air cover.

I used to tell the team that my job was to take out the people trying to cause them problems by taking them off course and creating challenges. My job was to try to make sure we were creating an environment where they didn't feel that I was giving them mistaken directions or that they were having to betray their other bosses.

I gave them air cover by working collaboratively with their direct line of business leaders to ensure that everybody was on the same page. Even today, I bring in all my leaders for a big decision. It may appear to be specific around finance, but I need the operating team and the marketing team to understand it so I can get their buy-in that we are all working toward the same goal.

THE TEAM

Patience and keeping the teams on the ground and back home motivated and optimistic are keys to unlocking a final deal.

Getting the right team is essential. At Disney, the previous deal teams had been senior executives who didn't have the time to invest in the relationship with Shanghai because they were running other parts of the company. I wanted a team that could go and live there, and the general counsel or the master planner were never going to do that.

Long-term partnerships can require longer negotiation, especially when you have cultural and political obstacles to overcome either within your own company or within a country. Patience and keeping the teams on the ground and back home motivated and optimistic are keys to unlocking a final deal. Everyone needs to be invested and feel responsible. It's no good if the deal team is celebrating and no one at home feels like they are involved. You need an overall integrated team that feels good about the end result.

Disney executives were reluctant to send us to live in China, but I pointed out that we'd spent two decades trying to do a deal and the way we were trying clearly did not work. My experience in

Japan, Singapore, Malaysia, and other parts of the world had convinced me that the kind of relationships we needed couldn't be built if you were jetting in on Tuesday night and leaving again on Friday.

I brought in lawyers I had worked with in Japan who had good international experience, a lot of patience, and a lot of understanding of how to take Disney legal speak and translate it for other cultures. I tapped my own business development team, whom I had confidence in for their ability to think broadly and drive work without egos. I brought in a master planner who was new to Disney.

We took six folks from the United States to live there, and two lawyers from Japan and Hong Kong. In the end, when the Imagineering team came to help with the master planning, we had ten people staying in the Marriott Executive Apartments for two or three weeks in any given month, depending on holidays and so on. The team was complemented by a half a dozen Chinese interpreters, and a couple of managers living in China.

Everyone had subject-matter expertise, an ability to dedicate their time, an ability to understand how to translate Disney internationally, and some ability to understand Chinese culture.

If you would have asked the senior leaders in the Walt Disney Company who three quarters of those people were, including myself, they probably wouldn't have known. We weren't the A Team. We called ourselves the No-Name Team, because none of the people were necessarily at the top of their areas in Disney.

There's a perception that having the senior-most people is the way to build a successful deal team. It doesn't work like that. Senior leaders in companies don't always have the time to check the boxes you need to make a deal. There are exceptions, of course, but when I look at the teams I've had success with, they've usually been mid-level leaders with drive and passion, expertise, and the respect of their respective line-of-business areas. They are credible people, so integrating them into the team gives you credibility instantly.

Whereas senior leaders can't invest the time because they have broader responsibilities, your team needs to be able to align their specific task with the overall strategy.

The No-Name Team did exactly that. They understood the goal, they were passionate and creative in finding solutions that weren't about ego. They were willing to build relationships. They enjoyed immersing themselves in the culture. They wanted to see a new chapter in Disney's fairytale come to life. They took great pride in that. The level of buy-in we got because they understood the impact they could have on a society like China, giving something enjoyable back to them, was really important.

It created a team type of mentality. It was always "us," not "them," and certainly not "me." They didn't always agree with me, of course, and they didn't always like the decisions I made, but in the end, it was always "us." I greatly appreciated that.

Success doesn't come from winning every battle. It comes from understanding the final goal and making each step count in getting there. Teams need appreciation. They need to have someone help connect the dots between what they're doing and the final outcome. And they need to feel accountable for the finished product or, in this case, the final deal.

When you get the right people on the plane, you can fly anywhere and be successful. That's how I felt about the team that we took to China and other teams that I've led for Disney and for Four Seasons. That's true even if you're just going to a different state. If you've got the right team on the plane, you can be successful anywhere you land.

Michael and colleagues in the steam rising from a hotpot dinner in Harbin eaten in an igloo made entirely of ice.

CONNECT THE TEAM WITH THE ULTIMATE GOAL

I told the team at the outset, "We're going to do the right thing no matter what that means. You're never wrong to do the right thing."

I warned them to be prepared for tension and told them that

the deal was either going to work, in which case we'd be celebrated for the accomplishment, or there would be a lot of bumpy roads and no one could begin to tell what our jobs would be like afterward.

I think everybody bought into the idea that I had the right approach to make decisions and get things done. By then, I had a track record of living internationally and making deals. I had experience in building relationships and trust. That helped people believe that I knew what I was talking about.

One thing I always did was to connect what the team was doing with the ultimate goal. It's easy when you're running a marathon to get overwhelmed thinking, *I have to run twenty-six miles*. You have to celebrate every one of the miles that add up to twenty-six. I made a point of celebrating every milestone so the team could see the progression in what we had achieved. We did benchmarking and took moments away to try to remember what the ultimate goal was. There was a lot of skepticism that this was never going to get done. Then in about month fourteen, people back in the United States started to change their minds.

That shift in attitude was pure energy for the team. We all felt a sea change and started to gain real momentum. In any deal, momentum is key. When you feel it working for you, the team starts to work harder and feels more energized and all of that translates into results. It was mainly small wins, as always, but we could feel that we were getting there.

As the team started to see the goal line, believe it or not, even after almost two years, they started to work harder. The hours got longer because people really believed that the ultimate result would have an impact for our company and an impact on people's lives. And an impact on them as individuals. That kind of momentum got everyone involved in what was being accomplished.

MAKE SURE YOU BRING IN THE RIGHT EXPERTISE

I often think that people are too wired to focus on what's next. I always tell my daughter to appreciate the moments as you live in them.

In big deals, you need to stay in the moment and not skip ahead. You have to take the steps and go through the education to set yourself up for long-term success. You don't want surprises a year or two years into negotiations. "Gosh, I wish we would've thought of that," or "I wish we'd taken more time to learn about the environment that we were going into or the laws or the culture."

It takes time to develop expertise, which is why companies need a team that's willing to invest personally. They have to bring their own expertise but also understand the sacrifices they'll make by being away from family and friends. They have to be able to strike a balance that will set up a long-term partnership. They need a willingness to understand how you take your product and make it culturally relevant in a place that might be very different.

Expertise gives you credibility at the deal table and trust within your own organization. If your organization doesn't trust that you know what you're doing, you're not going to have the backing you need to make decisions.

The Chinese really respect expertise. It's like playing poker. If you bluff, they know. And they do their homework to find out about you and your biography. They investigate what you've done and where you've been. They verify your credentials and dig into your subject-matter expertise. They knew things about me I don't think I ever told them.

Having a great team was the only way we could get it done. This was never going to be a one-man show. It needed a team that could feel good about what they were doing and empowered about getting things done.

The team was usually made up of people who only reported to me for the deal but reported to somebody else for their actual job. Our marketing person reported to a marketing manager and so on. For every single line of business, there was a tried and true method back in the United States, so that line-of-business leader was going to question everything we did. I had to hire credible people from their line of reporting so my team members would be able to say to the head of marketing, "What Michael is saying is actually right. I know how we did something else at Disneyland in California, but it won't work here."

The other piece of the puzzle was to find team members who would be intellectually curious about the culture and try to put what they did in the Chinese context. The way in which I led them was empowering but integrating, so they believed that I had the authority to do what I said I was able to do. The other side of the table had to believe that I had the authority. That depends on having people at the top of the company there to walk the walk and say the right words to establish your expertise. The top leadership at Disney came out and told the Chinese,

"*He's* the guy, and *that's* the team." Then when they left, the other side of the table said, "Okay, he's the guy."

And it was the same at Four Seasons.

A cultural immersion trip for the team to the Great Wall of China.

SHIFT INDIVIDUAL THINKING TO THE OVERALL GOAL

The goal when you're making a deal or running a company is always integrated decision making. That means you need to push people beyond themselves. You want to have them hearing each other's stories and opportunities and frustrations, so that if they have to give something up in negotiations to achieve the greater good, they understand it's not just them. They are part of a broader set of considerations. In the same way, people not directly involved also have to understand the broader decision-making process, so that individuals can avoid making decisions that might create difficulty in achieving the overall goal.

Pushing individuals to think beyond what was on their own page and consider the entire story was really important. Someone might feel it was like a loss to, say, give up 0.5 percent of a tax… but that might get us land for one hundred years rather than fifty years. I pushed them to think beyond their specific area to doing the best deal possible for the whole company. And sharing information helps them have more confidence at the deal table that they know what they're talking about.

I always had their back, though I also asked them to make sure they communicated with me before they got too far out on a limb. It might snap off.

I didn't want people to worry about making decisions. You have to make 100 decisions today. If you don't, there's 150 tomorrow or 200 the next day. It might feel uncomfortable, but if you don't make the decisions, we can't get this done. It's as simple as that. So I pushed people to have more confidence to make decisions. I pushed them to see beyond, "Hey, I'm just here to figure out what the land cost is gonna be" or "I'm just here to design a ride." They weren't only there for that. They were a part of something bigger that had to be great, so they couldn't view themselves as an unconnected individual or a siloed specialist.

IT'S ABOUT PEOPLE *AND* PROCESS

A lot of negotiators are people persons because it's harder for people who are not to gain trust from the other side. A people person benefits from having a process person to support them, however, to help ensure that the structure, the timelines, and the goals are aligned. Ideally, success is less about being a people person than it is about being someone who is well-rounded enough to understand the importance of relationships and building trust in your team and with your potential new partner. It's someone who does not arrive with an ego about preventing the other side from having opportunities.

As leader, I had to be able to manage relationships internally and externally to get the team to move in a unified direction. If the other side doesn't believe you're there to help them as much as you are there to help yourselves, the relationship is doomed to fail. The team has to have complete confidence in you. The company has to have complete confidence in you. The other side of the table has to have complete confidence in your influence and your ability to orchestrate the right outcome.

You may not always have the answer, but don't be afraid of asking questions that may look naive to find the answer. Again, that can involve giving up a little ego, but you have to inspire confidence because your team members are outside the normal operating environment they're used to being in. That makes them less confident about what they can or can't do on behalf of the company.

At both Four Seasons and Disney, we had a highly organized and rigorous process for managing deals. We had someone scheduling meetings. We had someone following up and tracking open items that needed to be resolved. We had reports and communication going back to other line of business leaders and senior leaders. We had regular reports that set milestones to work toward so that we could check on whether we were making the progress we needed to continue to get the deal done. We had big quarterly meetings that laid out our progress, where we were, and our milestones, so that everyone felt included.

One of the potential chokepoints, for example, is the legal process. It's there to prepare for the worst possible outcomes, but the danger is that when you marry legal issues with business issues, everything simply stops. If you don't keep checking progress, you could run a deal process forever. You could analyze and overanalyze every stage to a point where you could talk yourself out of doing the things that would allow you to make progress.

TEAM SPIRIT

You have to take moments with each of the constituent groups to celebrate the wins and keep them motivated so everyone feels part of what's going on.

While negotiations were going on, there was little time to socialize. We'd be in sessions all day then come back home and have the daily working-team lead meeting at 5:30 or 6:00 p.m. We would all get in a conference room at the Marriott Executive Apartments and compare notes on what had happened during the day.

I was the glue, because I was the one person who knew everything that was going on. I'd remind everyone about key points from the day in case somebody on one of the other teams needed to hear them. We finished up at 7:00 or even 9:00 p.m., ate dinner, and then prepared for the next day.

I made sure I organized something social on a weekly basis. It might be drinks or dinner, or going to listen to a band. When things got really intense, we'd go for the weekend to a different location in China or Asia to try to understand tourism from a different point of view. That kind of trip was really good for morale and team building but also allowed us to see the other types of hotels and tourist activities we were competing with.

A traditional village the team visited in Lijiang, China, part of the Yunnan Province.

If there was something big in a team member's life, like a child's birthday or a wedding anniversary, or a sick relative at home, I'd tell them, "Get on the plane, go." That helped the team feel very connected. The others had them covered and picked up the slack, which created a cohesive unit.

Once a month, we all came back to the States to update other people at home, and we all had regular calls. You may come across instances where your corporate teams are less flexible, given their geography and their normal MO for conducting business. If you're in a different time zone from HQ, it's you who needs to be prepared for late night calls or early morning calls. That's simply expected. I always tried to equal that out for the teams as much as possible by saying, "Hey, if we do one late night call, you have to do one early morning, or vice versa." Sometimes it worked...and sometimes not.

There were days where people felt run down and wondered whether it would ever end. Then we'd have a breakthrough and we'd all go out to the Filipino karaoke bar to celebrate.

We had dinner one night in an American restaurant and bar called the Blue Frog. They had something called the Wall of Fame, and the guy at the top was named Disney. I asked somebody, "What is this?" They said, "Well, we sell a hundred different kinds of shots. We give you a little passport book to keep track, and if you do all hundred shots you get your name up on the wall."

I told the team, "I've found the thing that we have to do."

A group of us said, "We're going to do this," and it became a team-building thing. We'd go to the place once a week, get a burger and do three or four shots, some of which were quite simple and others very complex. We'd come back the next week and do it all over again. By the end, we all got our names up on the wall.

I still have my passport book.

Those kinds of things helped the team have fun at times where it was really difficult. And it was all because the guy's name was Disney. I told the team, "It's a sign."

Mike and members of the team with the Wall of Fame in the Blue Frog cocktail bar, topped by Robert G. Disney.

Team spirit isn't only about the team directly involved with the deal, however. It was also about the team that was indirectly involved and the team sitting across the table, too. You have to take moments with each of those constituent groups to celebrate the wins and keep them motivated so everyone feels part of what's going on. I'd send folks at home videos or give them a chance to weigh in on certain decisions. And at the quarterly meetings or other one-on-one meetings, I was always fully prepared to report to each person that had anything to do with the deal, directly or indirectly, with a level of detail that made sure they felt respected, because feeling respected is what creates spirit and advocacy.

BE PREPARED FOR THINGS YOU DIDN'T ANTICIPATE

As a leader and as a team, you have to be prepared for anything that comes along. Obstacles will get put in the road. You can't prevent that, but you can decide how you choose to maneuver around them, go over them, or take them out. You have to be open and honest with the team that you're going to encounter things you can't anticipate at the outset. You're also going to learn more as you go through the process about what's important to the other side.

You have to have the right mentality not to be overcome. It might be unexpected, but that doesn't mean it should be a huge surprise. It's like playing football. You have a game plan, but two plays in, the other team does something you didn't think they were going to do. You have to make changes.

If you don't have the ability to make changes, you can't get things done. That's true in any situation.

BE AN OPEN BOOK

It's taken working around the world to prepare me for my current role back in my home state of Ohio, working for Hall of Fame Resort & Entertainment Company. It's on a smaller scale, but it still has the same challenges. It's still dealing with government. It's still dealing with politics and bureaucrats. It's still dealing with community and the perception that you're taking away resources that could be used for something else. You're still trying to help people understand the strategic value of building a unique destination in a particular location.

When I look back on doing this in places like Tokyo or Toronto, or other places around the world, it's always the same story. People go through a process a little like the stages of grieving. There's denial, when they ask, "Why do we need to do this?" There's anger and questioning and depression, then finally comes acceptance. Just like anywhere else, you use trust to build relationships. It's no different in Ohio than anywhere else. People have to understand what they're signing up for.

One of the things the board said when they recruited me for this job was, "We know this may not make any sense, but we want you to live in Canton, Ohio." I said, "Why do you think that doesn't make any sense? I'm from Ohio. It's like a wolf pack there. You're either with us or you're not, and if you are then you live here, you go through the winters, you pay our taxes. You're part of our community. If you're not with us, you're living out in Los Angeles and you're flying in once a month."

It's exactly the same as I'd seen in Shanghai.

It took me about three seconds to agree. The people in Ohio had

had a lot of promises made and none of them had been fulfilled, so why would they trust me if I wasn't a part of the community? I have to look people in the eye every day. This is a community where I still have relatives a half hour away asking me, "How is it going to work? Is it going to work?" I'm on the news a lot and in the press a lot. Doing a deal for Disney in Shanghai brought some pressure—but it's nothing compared to doing a deal in the place you grew up, with your mother, your aunt, and everybody else asking you how it's going.

Mike as a baby on his mother's lap, with his father (left) and maternal grandparents.

Geography varies and many things change, but ultimately it all comes back to the same thing: people acting from common values, with common successes and common failures. You have to have trust. It can be more difficult to establish trust in a geography with different points of reference, or when you don't speak the same language, but people everywhere inherently want to trust what you're telling them.

I came back to Ohio and had breakfast with one of the county commissioners. She said to me, "I can tell you're from Ohio." I laughed and said, "Oh yeah, how's that?" She says, "Just from how plain spoken you are. You're not trying to sell me on something. You're not trying to manipulate me into doing something. You're just telling me what it is that's going on."

My philosophy is not to hide anything. It's all an open book. You want to understand the numbers? Here's the numbers. You think I'm hiding something? Have your lawyers take a look, have your finance team take a look. What good does it do me to lie to you and then three years later meet you at the local grocery store where you say, "Hey buddy, you told me one thing and now it's something different."

I always encourage people to do business by being open and honest and professional. If you let people know the challenges you're going through, it helps you stay humble. You won't have all the answers and your team needs to know that it's okay to say, "I don't know." You might have the best-laid plan, but your team needs to know it's okay that they will fail on a decision here or there as long as, in the end, everyone appreciates having made a contribution to the success you have. Too often, people approach new deals in new locations as a chance to try to maneuver to get a better deal or to create a different image. Especially in Asia, there's not a chance. You can know everything. You can study. You can learn. You can get the expertise. Something is going to come up that you didn't sign up for.

All you can do is be ready.

RELATIONSHIPS FOR LIFE

It was a leap of faith to ask potential members of the team to step sideways off what they were doing in Disney for something that might not come off. I used two arguments. Number one, any time the CEO of the Walt Disney Company tells you he views it as his personal legacy to take the company into China, and that getting the theme park and resort division there is one of the most important initiatives for the entire company, that's pretty easy motivation—even though it's intimidating. Number two, doing business internationally will expand your mind and expand your capabilities for the future. Disney had made it very clear that international growth was a priority for the company, so this could grow and develop them as professionals and really help their careers in the future. Both those things turned out to be true.

Because I had been a part of three or four different opening teams for new destinations, I told the team, "You won't believe how close you're going to get. You'll never forget the friendships you make in this team. Everybody supports everybody else. You will be with people that you will have a relationship with for the rest of your life."

Last year, that whole team came together to celebrate the tenth anniversary of the deal. Everyone cares about each other and is still involved with each other's lives.

When the Imagineers arrived, we wanted to make sure they had the right attitude and the right thought process. I included a couple of people from the Imagineering team in the deal process so that they understood how different it was going to be to do business in China. The Imagineering team had proven success in many creative disciplines, and they could just have sent whomever, but we told them they had to select people like the deal team: people with creative expertise in their field, but who could also live in China, understand cultural differences, and set their egos aside to listen to others.

Working with your team is like going into battle. You have to trust each other and value each other. You need to feel that everyone is going through the same challenges and overcoming the same difficulties together—and that spirit creates a value proposition that you can't imagine if you haven't experienced it before.

The same holds true as an expat living outside the geographies where you live most of your life. You find yourself becoming friends with people not just on your team but in the community that you may never have been friends with otherwise. Everyone has an "all in it together" mentality. They are learning and sharing, and they want everyone to be successful. I think people genuinely take more of an interest in others in a situation like that.

We had that special bond in Shanghai. I had it in situations with Four Seasons. I have it today in my own company. I've built a team and we're creating destinations, creating gaming, creating media. Everything is new—and we're getting to put our thumbprints on it.

That idea came from ancient builders who put their handprints or fingerprints into soft clay or concrete in Egypt and elsewhere. And twenty years from now, we will be able to go back and show our kids or friends what our team achieved. "Look at what we did."

People want to make a difference and have an impact. It's a little like the reason I'm writing this book for people who might be going through the same things I went through. And the relationships you build while you're doing it, either directly or indirectly with others in the community, are invaluable. They are what help you survive the times that you think are going to be the most difficult.

REFRAME ANY LOSSES

People on the deal get upset about things that go wrong because they have so much vested in the deal happening. If you miss out on one of your big asks, it can be crushing. From the beginning, you try to tell people that if they believe they're going to win every single point in the negotiations, they're wrong. They have to understand that they won't get in trouble for losing points. It's a game of compromise, and everyone needs to be aligned to deliver the best possible product.

The feeling of loss can be terrible. If you're really pushing hard for something and you have to compromise, it feels awful. That is only natural. When I sensed that happening, I would bring everybody back and say, "Let me repaint this picture for you. Remember that point? We got it exactly the way we wanted. Remember this one? We got exactly what we needed on that, too. Remember these other two that we never thought were going to be something that we could get close to? We got three quarters of those things. Why are we so worried about this one thing?"

People understand that attitude. But if you see doing a deal only in terms of wins and losses, for you to win, somebody else has to lose. That's one thing if you're trying to beat somebody in a game of football, but deals are partnerships. You're not trying to have more wins than your partners. You're trying to overcome obstacles in a holistic way so that if there are any decisions people perceive as losses, they also understand that they are necessary. It's a compromise that will lead to a stronger outcome.

Sometimes you have to be very literal about these things when you're giving guidance to your headquarters or your negotiating counterpart: "Look, I'm willing to do this because it will get us much closer to this outcome. This gives us a much better chance of a stronger, long-term partnership for your company as well as mine." It's worth taking the time to explain that giving in or compromising on a particular decision doesn't mean that you're losing. It means you're making something better come out of it. If you can get people to understand that, they have a much different attitude.

NO ONE LEFT BEHIND

People working internationally usually believe either that they don't have to change anything to be successful or that they have to change everything.

If someone thinks they are just a representative of the company who is there to say, "This is what we've done successfully, so we'll do it again," they are not empowered. Their only motivation is that they've been given an assignment that might help their career. They are desperate not to screw it up, so they make sure they're never perceived as doing something against the company's interests or processes. They worry that they won't have a job in the main company to go back to.

The risk is always that people who have had success in their particular field of expertise believe they know exactly what they bring to the table. They believe they will have success if they bring exactly the same thing to the next deal. They worry that if they change, their counterparts in the corporate headquarters might perceive them as going rogue or local.

No one wants to be in that position.

In cases like that, deal leaders have to give them air cover. They have to say, "Look, these individuals are evolving. They're changing their thinking based on advice and cultural immersion and the situation on the ground. Sometimes we have to give to get, and those gives are not losses."

Individuals have to feel like they have room to evolve their thinking based on what they learn, and that they're not going to be doubted or kicked aside if they don't give the answers the corporate headquarters or the board expects. Everything changes when you're living in another geography, when you're dealing with other companies, when you're involved in situations that are impacted by the stock market or the supply chain or other unpredictables. It's important to have the ability to assure people they won't be kicked to the curb if they don't always do what's expected, as long as they have built their opinions on benchmarks and facts.

Sometimes I see people fail to support their hypothesis with the right information, the right facts, the right consultants, the right lessons. That's when their company or board, or their colleagues, perceive them to not be acting in the company's best interest.

When I chose the team to go to Shanghai, I chose people who had done a great job at what they'd already been asked to do in their careers. That gave the company trust. Then when those people got to be boots on the ground, they started realizing life was going to be different where they had arrived. Everything was different.

The people still back in North America didn't realize that because they hadn't had those experiences. That's why I got them to come over and spend quality time in cultural immersion, rather than just business meetings.

Over time, if people are away from the office, companies tend to forget that they sent those people to represent them because of their greatness. Businesses should trust that those people have the ability to help evolve their product in a significant way. But it's a two-way street. Those individuals have the responsibility of making sure that they strengthen and increase trust through their communication, their education, their cultural respect.

The other way companies make mistakes is that they let people get lost. They send them on supposedly high-profile overseas assignments, but then they forget about them. When someone who has been in Paris for eight years says, "Hey, I want to come back to the United States because my folks are getting older and everyone I know is back there," too many companies say, "Gosh, I don't know what we have for you. Maybe you will have to take a demotion or maybe you have to come back and prove yourself to us all over again."

The situation has changed a little because technology allows more regular connectivity, but the danger is that you get a lower quality product because people are afraid that doing or saying anything different will mean they are left behind. They're not in the meetings that everybody else is in every single day. They have no idea what people at home are saying about their deal or their future. And like everyone else, when they don't know something, they start imagining the worst...

CHAPTER 6

Working in Asia

GOING INTERNATIONAL

> It amazes me when companies set out to do business in Asia by repeating what they do elsewhere in the world. That approach simply cannot work.

It sometimes feels as if virtually every company wants to expand its business overseas, particularly in Asia. The surprising thing is that so many of them arrive in a new geography completely unprepared. They have a lot of aha moments and surprises, and they spend a lot of time saying, "Gee, I didn't know that." It might be the tax environment, the HR environment, the workforce environment, or the ability to control supply chains in a more reliable fashion. They haven't done their due diligence.

STRUCTURE SHOULD ACCOUNT FOR TRANSFERRED LESSONS

Even sophisticated companies try to enter new markets on the cheap by simply applying the lessons they learned from other markets. If you've done something in four other markets and it's worked, that can help, for sure. But if you don't have boots on the ground to make sure you understand the nuances of doing business in this particular geography, you'll lose out.

Disney had never put someone in charge of the overall operation on the ground as early as they did with me in Shanghai. They knew I had the history and the relationships to build trust with new people as they came in—the deal team, the design and construction team, the operating team—and guide them so they didn't misstep. Having been the guy on the ground who had to pick up where the developers left off, I always made sure to have early and constant input from whoever would run the project after a deal was done. That way, I become the thread of consistency from the time we start to form the relationship for the deal to the time the destination opens.

A presentation to mark Mike as he leaves Business Development to become Head of Shanghai Disney Resort.

A lot of companies don't think that way. They send a business development team to do a deal to build a new manufacturing plant in, say, Korea. They hire some Koreans to build it, then a couple of months before the plant opens, they bring over their own people to figure out how to run it. And that's when they start to realize that operating a business in Korea is very different than operating in Vietnam. And by then it's too late. Building core knowledge in a business will help a lot—but it still comes as a surprise that Japan doesn't work like China or Vietnam doesn't work like Malaysia. What works in Shanghai might not even work in Beijing.

Building any physical infrastructure without operational input and understanding is almost guaranteed to bring extra cost once the key players turn up and tell you what they actually need. Companies avoid it because it slows development down and perhaps costs a little more to get operational input up front. I've seen a lot of companies kick that can down the road. "We know it's an issue, but let's leave it for the operational team to sort out later."

STRONG RELATIONSHIPS ARE OFTEN UNDERVALUED

There's always a price to doing business in other countries—but it's not always about money.

What Four Seasons did better than most companies was realize that if they didn't invest in and manage the relationships with the people who owned their hotels, they would risk product quality, service quality, and the potential for overall brand degradation. I had deep admiration for their founder Isadore Sharpe, a gentleman I considered the best at making you feel like you were the most important person in a room, no matter who else was there and what else was going on. His philosophy of treating others as you would want to be treated clearly translated to the individual teams running the hotels as well. The relationship that Four Seasons employees have with their guests is unmatched. Many companies do not take relationship management to the individual level when managing their team or doing deals with other partners. They don't think about what's important to the other side of the table when trying to determine key terms for a long-term partnership.

When I arrived in Singapore, my biggest goal was to take that relationship management and evolve it to be even more efficient and responsive to owner needs. I wanted to execute it in ways that were culturally relevant and respectful of individual geographies. I wanted to be more present and build relationships around trust. I hadn't been with the Four Seasons company very long, but I was given the authority to effect real change and oversee all disciplines to help expedite growth. It was a new role in the company, and I had to leverage all the lessons I had already learned about communication, balancing needs from a corporate perspective with different owners' needs in unique geographies throughout Asia.

I was lucky to have had the support from the CEO and the board, but there was still skepticism around a new role having the autonomy to challenge the status quo. There were many instances when I had to ask for resources or change an investment strategy or operating procedure to something that was slightly different than what had been done in the past. I took the time to invest in building relationships prior to making changes. Building advocacy and bringing partners into the tent is critical to success in business and in life. I was fortunate that I was working for a company that recognized the need to change their approach to manage the growth targets they had set for a very important part of the world like Asia.

As I transitioned to become head of portfolio management, I kept that same mentality. In my new global role, I valued relationships and always tried to balance the needs of the Four Seasons company with those of the new owner, resort, or hotel—or even the regional teams that already had great success in developing trusting relationships in other parts of the world. I worked to support key issues that may have been difficult for them to deal with directly without impacting their established relationships. There's always a need to "level up" support, and I looked at my job in part as providing a different perspective to the owners and to the internal stakeholders of the company. Not always a popular position to hold, but when you have the trust of your team, your company, and your counterparts, there's usually a way to bridge the gap.

The same was true with my time at Disney. Shanghai was the ultimate test of relationship building and relationship management.

A cultural dinner with Four Seasons owners in Asia.

AN OVERSEAS OFFICE CAN SERVE AS AN INCUBATOR FOR NEW IDEAS

As tastes develop and as education takes place, the market keeps evolving. Shanghai Disney Resort had to keep changing because the Chinese are always looking for something different. Some pieces of your product are evergreen. They don't change. But the softer pieces—programming, food, merchandise—have to constantly evolve based on customer demand. Five years ago, you'd go to a hotel and say "I want the best hamburger and fries." Now it's, "I want the best salad because I'm focused on nutrition and carbon footprint."

Running a company outside of where every other asset was placed is like running an incubator. You learn customs and habits that allow you to educate the rest of the company. Some things only make sense in a specific country, but others are universal. Walt Disney World Resort can't tailor its experience only for the Chinese because the British, the Mexicans, the Germans, and the French are all coming. Each resort combines local elements with elements that are universally appealing.

We would do annual retreats with all of Disney's senior leaders to discuss the nuances of running the business in particular places around the world. Information was shared that would be taken back to the other businesses. Everyone might have the same button on a website, but it might get placed a little differently here or there, depending on what people expected. That kind of education is gold for any global company. When I was global head of portfolio management at Four Seasons, that was the kind of thing I would search out.

Create a group of consultants or internal stakeholders you

can trust to inform you about global trends and preferences. That allows you to proactively engage to continue to grow your market share. We brought in consultants based in China, like Mercer or Deloitte, who were all Chinese people speaking fluent English because they had been educated at reputable schools in the United States to the UK, or in other high-profile educational institutions from around the world. There is a churn of highly skilled people who can speak the languages and who know the culture. They have a foot in both camps.

We also hired local talent with the experience to bring our understanding of nuance to a different level. The key is, you have to listen to them. Once you've brought them on board, create a safe environment for them to challenge the normal way you do business in other places. It makes no sense to create an opportunity to learn from local people and then spend your time forcing them to conform to how you do business elsewhere.

BUSINESS IN CHINA

The other side of doing business in China is that a lot of the laws are new and untested. Questions remain around longevity and how the country will evolve.

It's not possible to operate in China unless the Chinese want you to. The decision to reopen negotiations about Shanghai Disney coincided with the Chinese taking a new attitude toward theme parks. The Chinese classify types of companies or developments in various ranks, from "encouraged" all the way down to "prohibited." Theme parks were on the not-encouraged list because they eat land, which means upsetting farmers or other industries. In the past, the Chinese government never understood the value of theme parks to attract tourism, but that changed in the mid-2000s, when they started to see parks as a way to contribute to what they called "quality of life." They decided that a theme park could help improve the quality of life for the mainland Chinese, and for Shanghai.

They watched cities like Tokyo, Paris, London, Singapore, and Los Angeles become meccas for tourism, and they began to appreciate what a huge economic driver tourism can be. People come to your city, they spend a lot of money, and they leave. You don't have to increase your infrastructure. You don't have to add more police or schools, because the tourists go home.

Disney could never have built the park on its own because the company was on the non-recommended development list, so we had to work with the government. That creates a lot more flexibility because the government can make new rules about construction and operations there. Shanghai was an obvious location for all the reasons you would expect. Pudong, on the edge of the city, was an economic development zone, so from a regulatory standpoint, there was a lot more flexibility because the government could make new rules about construction there. The Shanghai government wanted a way to help Pudong grow; they viewed Shanghai Disney Resort as a way to drive traffic away from the main city and bring it to Pudong.

If you're doing business that requires land, don't turn up with too much certainty of where you want to be. The Chinese will tell you where they're happier for you to be. For a hotel, they can likely find space downtown, but a manufacturing plant will be pushed out into the urban sprawl to provide jobs for the growing population. The Shanghai government was expert at master planning for the city, and developing an overall strategic plan for growth that allowed new infrastructure to be developed in key areas so that others could gain citizenship to help the population grow, to have the appropriate workers, and to maintain a balance in growth between manufacturing, finance, leisure, and tourism.

THE COST OF DOING BUSINESS IN CHINA CAN BE HIGH

Decades ago, mainland China did generous deals to incentivize companies to move there if the companies had IP or technical knowledge around a specific business that China wanted to grow. In the late 1990s and 2000s, that started to change. China went from a baby to a small child to an adolescent in terms of world trade. The Chinese realized they were movers and shakers and developed more of a sense of pride. Their attitude became, "You need us more than we need you. You need to be here to be exposed to well over a billion people whose income is increasing at double-digit growth and who can buy your goods or services. If you're not here, that's a giant hole." In the early 2000s, the rallying cry of most businesses around the world was, "We have to get into mainland China."

They soon learned that the roadmap to figuring out China was much more difficult than originally expected. The regulatory environment, the banking environment, and the tax environment were all so complicated for foreign companies that it made the cost of doing business astronomical. Companies have to understand every aspect of the business. We hired Ernst & Young to advise us on taxes. We hired construction and industry consultants to advise us on how to source materials, which was more complex and expensive than anyone had thought.

Everyone thought things in China would be cheaper, but the market matured quickly. It's inevitable. Look at economic history. Manufacturing started in Europe. Then unions began to take hold and labor became expensive, so manufacturing moved to America. The same happened again, so manufacturing moved to Mexico. Then to China. Companies tend to focus on the huge workforce in China; they don't realize that a huge workforce brings huge costs every time you give them a raise or better healthcare. Costs rose exponentially in China, which is why manufacturing is moving to Vietnam, Taiwan, and other places.

It always happens that having more income-qualified consumers comes at the cost of having the price of doing business go up. Companies started to pay workers more, so business costs started to accelerate, in some places faster than anyone could have imagined. Economic performance built on cheap labor suffered because companies first had to pay more to get the right mainland Chinese talent with the right background, meaning they had worked for a Western company or had been educated in the UK, the US, or Canada and had come back to China to build a career.

The other side of doing business in China is that a lot of the laws are new and untested. Questions remain around stability and how the country will evolve. Whereas more mature countries have dependable legal systems based on precedent, China doesn't always have precedent. Many land deals haven't yet reached maturity, for example, and the tariffs placed on imports and exports haven't stabilized.

Risk is simply part of what you must endure. You can mitigate it as much as you possibly can, but you can't solve every problem. If you stop and let lawyers imagine all of the worst possible things that can happen, you will never get agreement. You'd have terms so onerous that no one would sign them. I like to provide for a way to have conversations with your partner in the future by creating dispute resolution mechanisms.

The lack of maturity and instability around the legal system makes it more important to give yourself ways to resolve bumps in the road.

DOING BUSINESS IN CHINA ISN'T ROCKET SCIENCE

Somewhere like China might be different from what you're used to, but it's not *that* different. If you take the time to study the business environment, it's not a mystery at all. The Chinese are all very open about it: "This is how we operate."

The starting point is to take the time to think about what is really important to you, to your company, your brand, your product, or your service. Then think about what is really important to whomever it is you're trying to form a partnership with.

Figure out where the marriage can occur—and if it can't, don't do the deal. Even if it's worth a lot of money, it won't be successful.

The key for me was respecting the Chinese terms. Simply put, don't walk into somebody else's home wearing your shoes when you know that they don't allow shoes to be worn in their home. That's disrespectful. The Chinese have their own footwear-related saying: "Walk in our shoes." What they mean is, "Stop looking at it from only your side. You can't make a one-sided deal, so think about it from our perspective. You may not like it, but you're going to have to give."

There is no win for one side or the other. There is only compromise and cooperation. If you can achieve those two things to the satisfaction of your business, that's a heck of a lot better outcome than some. When Uber went over to China, the government allowed a Chinese company to knock off what Uber was doing. They told Uber, "Sorry, we're backing this company instead."

Of course, Disney wasn't a pharmaceutical company or a car manufacturer. The Chinese weren't going to kick us out and build another Disney. So there was no competition risk—but there was still brand risk and financial risk, and they were very real.

NEVER FORGET THAT CHINA IS NOT THE UNITED STATES

Lots of companies head to China or other places in Asia and try to replicate whatever they do that's made them successful at home. That involves making two huge errors.

Number one, you need to respect Chinese culture and how it works. The mistake I see most companies make is to think, "We have a formula that works, so we'll just translate it into Chinese." Being in the right language isn't enough. It also has to tick the box of being respectful of how their culture works. For example, does it acknowledge that more people walk rather than drive? Does a food or beverage respect the tastes they've grown up with? The Chinese like trying new things as much as anybody else, but they still expect things to be a little familiar.

Unlike many mature Western countries, including the United States, China still faces issues connected with the reacquisition of Hong Kong, tension with Taiwan, and China's close ties with

Russia. These factors bring a lot of instability not just to China but to the whole of Asia. Companies need to make a constant evaluation and reevaluation as they assess how to enter into Asia and China.

Number two, you need to satisfy the Chinese belief that they're different. They take a lot of pride in the idea that they have become a premier world power on many platforms. In Shanghai, the ticketing system was developed to allow Chinese visitors to use their national IDs because anything else was foreign to them. It doesn't matter where you are in the world: if you can create a connection to your product by using software or hardware people are familiar with, it will be a lot easier for them to adopt. It becomes part of something they're already using every day, as people use their cell phones to carry theater and sports tickets.

It was the same when we thought about a new Four Seasons in China or elsewhere in Asia. You take a hard look at what consumers are already doing, and you project how your product can connect with that in the future.

The Chinese want to feel they have something unique, whether it's the latest technology or different rides. Disneyland in California has Sleeping Beauty's Castle, while Walt Disney World Resort in Florida has Cinderella's Castle. Paris has Sleeping Beauty's Castle ("La Belle aux Bois") and in Tokyo, it's Cinderella's Castle again. Hong Kong initially had Sleeping Beauty's Castle, but it became the Castle of Magical Dreams, with a number of princesses. In Shanghai, we built the Enchanted Storybook Castle, where all the princesses lived together. It didn't have to be Chinese: it just needed to be different. They wanted something to brag about.

Mike and the Enchanted Storybook Castle in Shanghai, shortly after the opening of Shanghai Disney Resort.

Smart companies find a way to adapt their product so that it's still theirs, but theirs for China, with the appropriate packaging, imagery, and other distinct qualities. Our mantra in Shanghai was "Authentically Disney, distinctly Chinese." We looked for every angle to create an experience that would make a Westerner at the resort think, "Yeah, this is Disney," but would make a Chinese visitor say, "This feels very comfortable to me. It's entertaining and I'm seeing new and exciting things, but it's also familiar, so there's nothing I have to learn from scratch."

The key is in the details. We spent a lot of time doing consumer feedback sessions and understanding how we could translate every facet of our product operationally, creatively, and linguistically—so that it was relevant to consumers' lives but also presented something they'd never seen before that created a wow for them.

In Shanghai, the whole food and beverage program was catered to China, and so was the merchandise we sold. Japan was another example. Disney doesn't sell tatami mats in any other part of the world, but they sell them in Tokyo because visitors there sit on them during the parades.

Disney had had an office in Shanghai running consumer products and licensing, but they had less knowledge about resorts and parks, so we had to build that out. We developed a consumer website, and we invited people in to show them new merchandise or, say, a new ride. If they participated, they got a special coin or an invitation to an event; we used gamification to encourage their contribution.

The right cultural fit was important to retain employees. We focused on how we would recruit cast members with the right attitudes, the smiles, and the willingness to serve—because serving somebody else is not a job that a lot of people like if they see it as being subservient. We did a lot of testing with HR firms as to what motivated employees in China, and we learned that it was less about compensation and more about titles. The ability to progress in titles was very important so that when people went home for the Chinese national holidays, they could say to their parents or their friends, "I've been promoted." Most companies' traditional organizational pyramids might have a certain number of layers of seniority from the top to the bottom, maybe ten or twelve, so progress is slow. For companies in China, including those I have led, it is worth considering splitting those layers and increasing them dramatically to allow people to recognize their growth in the company. That allows for employee retention, even though it means smaller raises between different pay grades. The expectation of Chinese workers was, "I want to carry around a business card, and I want that business card to say something new on it every year or every two years."

A moderator conducts a focus group among Chinese locals to test new ideas and concepts for Shanghai Disney Resort.

People wanted to progress in their careers in ways similar to what we see in younger generations, like Millennials and Gen Z. Individuals are now interested in much faster career progression and growth, even if it doesn't come with meaningful monetary raises attached. They like to know there is a ladder that can be climbed that will give them the ability to grow their careers and show their family and friends the progress they make.

I hired Chinese consultants to do a full HR study for us so I could go back to corporate and say, "This is how we're going to do things differently." Doing things differently is no more popular inside Disney than in any other company. I told them, "This is a very unique environment."

We had to show that we were being distinctly Chinese by working on what was important for the people we hired. And we needed the right leadership team to articulate that story to show the parent company we weren't going rogue or going local. We had to convince the company to say, "We're okay with that change."

Like many companies, Disney arrived in China wanting to be able to display all of its products and services and to replicate models the company knew worked in other places around the world. But we had to learn to take a step at a time just like we did in the United States or other companies do wherever they're at. We didn't start with the entire line of products or services. We started with the theme park and resort. That gave us the opportunity to create a destination and tell stories. It gave us a foothold in the country with a physical presence that would gain us more momentum in the other business verticals, and hopefully a chance to grow them in the same way as had happened in the United States and other parts of the world.

To their credit, Disney's senior leaders listened, processed that, and understood. They got that we were starting from a point where we could develop a theme park and resort deal, and that would open the way for other parts of the company.

For the average Chinese involved in negotiation, their love and respect for—and their loyalty to—their country is greater than anyone's love for or loyalty to a company. It conditions virtually everything they do, and every action that they take.

We had to be careful not to put our own Chinese team interpreters and managers and others into a very difficult position. The saying was always "Chinese first." "Don't forget you are Chinese first."

THEY ARE CHINESE FIRST

Many times in my professional career, I've had Chinese or Japanese or people of other nationalities working for me who would say, "This is difficult for us because our country of origin is so important. We have so much national pride that some of what we're looking for in this deal is difficult for our country to do." That put them in a difficult situation, as it would with anybody. It would be the same if someone came into the United States and was looking to do something that was new and unique but didn't fit into the legal system the right way. Our first reaction as Americans would be, "Wow. I don't think we can do that. I don't think that the government will allow us to do that."

When I arrived in Shanghai, Disney had some local senior leaders as part of the team that had been part of the negotiation for many years. These leaders always advised us that from a Chinese perspective, it was much easier to give whatever the Chinese were asking for. The conflict between "Chinese first" and doing what was good for *both* sides made things so difficult that it became hard for Disney to trust these leaders' viewpoints.

When I arrived as the first more permanent set of boots on the ground, my observations and conclusions were naturally different from the ideas of the team that had been there for some time, because I was a Westerner and I had a different perspective. Those folks put a lot of emphasis on telling the company that this or that was the only way the Chinese government was going to allow the deal to be done. I wasn't so sure.

Like anyone working for companies that go to new locations where they have representation but no real corporate culture or US culture, I had to determine who would fit our strategy in the longer term. And when we started gathering information from other companies doing business in China, we learned a bunch of stuff that was very different than our guys had advised us. It became clear that their interests weren't always aligned with the company's interests.

We had our own interpreters who could read the room, see how the Chinese were thinking, and give us tips. We started to hire Chinese locals who could understand the nuances of the communication. There are times where interpreting is an art and the wording that came back to our side wasn't always exactly how it was intended. Whoever was negotiating on our side would say, "No, we can't do that" before one of our Chinese team members clarified things and said, "No, what they're trying to say is this, this, and this."

Mike hosts a dinner for Disney's local interpreters and support team, many of whom came from leading schools around the world.

We had a half a dozen or so cultural liaisons that advised us on how to interpret what was being said, literally and figuratively. That gave us a much more realistic view of what we needed to do and react to.

It turned out that the local leaders we let go had promised all of the existing Chinese in the Disney office roles in the project, even though many of them had no experience at all in that kind of thing. They had no experience as members of a negotiating team. We kept some doing their day jobs, but we made it clear we didn't need their support. We built our own team.

The lesson was clear: we had to form our own opinions on what we were being told. And the only way I was going to do that was by living there and developing my own relationships.

THINK ABOUT YOUR SUCCESSES AND FAILURES, NO MATTER WHERE

Believe me, the Chinese will look at what you've done in the past and use that to influence their regulations, financial contribution, or participation. They'll try to avoid repeating any failures you were involved in, but they'll also try to benefit from your success.

Take Google. The Chinese government didn't want Google to succeed because that would make information readily available to the mainland Chinese consumer that the government would prefer to limit. Take some of the pharmaceutical companies that went in to produce new or different types of drugs. The Chinese put their people right alongside them to learn so that knowledge transfer would ensure they had an ability to grow their own industries. The same thing happened in industries like auto-making, steel, and banking. China was really good at replication. They looked at success and imagined taking it to a whole new level.

The reality is that whatever you're doing in the world today, everyone has the ability to assess past performance. The bigger you are, the easier it is to assess. Around the world, companies will always look at your last deal or your previous operations and assess what they could do differently. They take a view on your failures and might try to leverage those to get better terms in a deal. You have to prepare when you go into a country to be able to address whatever issues that your company has faced in running an operation somewhere else. You can't be defensive. You have to own your failures.

Remember: if you were in the same situation as them, you would ask the same questions. Don't take offense, because everyone's simply trying to understand what's the best opportunity for success. And only when you're learning from your past can you really implement those lessons in a way that can be more meaningful in your future.

Of course, it's more difficult if your partner tries to apply past experience from different businesses or different partners or different cultures, such as applying lessons from France to a deal in China or experiences in Britain to business in Singapore.

Everyone has a different negotiating style and different outcomes they're looking for. Naturally, everyone wants to be profitable and successful, but when you start trying to apply lessons from different industries or different partners, it can create more chaos than good. We faced that in China, and I've faced it opening hotels and doing deals in other partnerships. All of this comes with baggage...and it is typically baggage that is brought on by others rather than by you.

So suddenly, you're dealing with a very cautious approach to doing business with you that's not even related to something your own company has done but to other deals by other businesses.

KEEP TABS ON OTHER DEALS

In China, most of the industries have some connection to government and many are state-owned entities (SOEs). That means they all share information on how different Chinese entities work with their foreign counterparts. They all have the latest information on the types of deals that have been struck.

Our Chinese counterparts would show up and start talking about different industries or specific companies, saying, "Here, this is what they've done." I had to start learning about other deals as a negotiating tactic. I went to different companies so I could say, "Look, I know that Goodyear does this. I know that Coca-Cola does this." I had to make sure we weren't asking them to do something for us they weren't already doing for other people. My counterparts appreciated that because it meant we weren't trying to embarrass them. I'd say, "We've investigated this, and this is what we've learned." Sometimes they would actually say, "Can you give us examples so that we can share with our leaders?"

I always did, because I appreciate that they have to have something to report to someone else. It's like they say, "Walk in each other's shoes." We're all in it together and everybody else is outside. You deal with your bosses, and I'll deal with my bosses.

DON'T EXPECT COMPLETE CONTROL

Everyone was initially nervous about working with the Chinese government. Disney's senior teams in marketing, public affairs, legal, and other departments were nervous about giving up control. They worried about creative control and operating integrity; they were worried about getting paid and moving money to the United States.

I remember one meeting where someone answered such criticism with a question: "What are the Chinese going to do? Roll tanks down the middle of Main Street?" It was never going to happen because in such a high-profile setting, that kind of action is unacceptable—and unthinkable. If the Chinese government did that to Disney, they'd destroy their credibility with other big brands. Who would want to operate there if they did that to one of the biggest brands in the world?

It was very much a partnership and the Chinese were making an investment as much as we were, so we assessed from the very beginning that this was a risk we were willing to take. Once we'd done that, it was much easier to make those kinds of decisions as the deal team proceeded to negotiate a final agreement.

The result was that Disney worked hard to balance out decision making and control within the partnership—but for me, that was another argument for making sure I got the Chinese interests aligned with our interests. That way, even if things got bad and they did things we might not like, they would have skin in the game, too. The face they presented to the world would be on the line as much as Disney's. I kept telling people that the Chinese were taking on as much risk bringing us in as we were taking in going there.

The government created Shanghai Shendi (Group) Co., Ltd., as a for-profit entity to partner with Disney, but the Shanghai Shendi management started to have their own ideas. This was when they wanted to build their hotels around the edge of the resort so they could start making money they didn't have to share with Disney. I suspect the deputy party secretary who ran Shanghai Shendi had visions of becoming something more than just a figurehead in a state-owned company. He wanted to build his own company, as he'd watched other Chinese leaders do.

Shanghai Shendi never told us what they were planning. We'd notice construction around the edge of the park and ask, "Do you know what that is?" and only then would they tell us. They never volunteered information. It was like being a prosecutor in court. If you didn't ask the questions, you didn't get the answers. We had to decide whether to have a battle to shut them down or to work with them to try to figure it out.

We decided to work with them, but it made me nervous. I had seen them take Google out of the country. I had seen them take over pharmaceutical companies after they learned everything about what they were doing. I worried they might eventually take us out of the country.

I reminded them, "We don't have the secret formula that will cure a disease, but we're still in business and we're making a considerable investment here in terms of our name and our money. If you start to compete with us in the early days, when people in China are still trying to figure out what a theme park is and why they would go there, it will just confuse them. You're competing for the same dollars as the hotels and restaurants you already have with us in the park."

They thought they had learned enough about how Disney did things to try to make some more money and have the best of both worlds. That was never the case. Disney had the bargaining power, the PR, the brand, even though that didn't suit the deputy secretary, who was trying to make his way upward in the Party.

The lesson for me is that you always have to ensure that your partner is aligned and doing what you both committed to. Be careful that they're not trying to get into the same space or an adjacent space off what they learn from you.

The Chinese have already learned to build their own theme parks. They have a group called Wanda that builds resorts and thrill-ride parks and smaller leisure destinations. They can see the value of developing the assets, but it's harder without the stories and the movies. Disney's premise was that if you create great content and tell great stories, people want to go and live in those three-dimensional worlds. So the Chinese either have to buy that content or create their own. So far, they've struggled with that level of creativity.

BE PREPARED TO HAVE YOUR PARTNER'S EMPLOYEES WITHIN *YOUR* ORGANIZATION

One of the things the Chinese insisted upon was placing people inside the organization. In the early days, that was a significant issue. They were proposing that Shanghai Shendi and its people would have some control of the overall operation, but I was reluctant to agree because that was the role Disney wanted me to fulfill.

The Chinese said, "Mike, you don't have people who understand Chinese culture, people who are Chinese that can communicate with the government. You guys can't do that, but we can. We'll be here to support you." I reminded them of their lack of familiarity with how a Disney operation runs. There couldn't be any control unless we had people with the right qualifications.

The compromise was to tell them, "You can't appoint people to these positions, but you can nominate them." That was a big difference from virtually every other company in China, where the Chinese counterpart simply appointed people into key positions. We told them, "We could be comfortable if you're saying that you need representation in the organization to make you feel comfortable. But you can't just force people on us because we're doing something that you don't really understand. We want to see their CVs. We want to interview them in the regular way. If they're not qualified, we get to say no."

We told them, "Your people have no idea how to run or account for a Disney resort. You can have representation, but they report to us through our organization, not to yours." I explained that we couldn't allow anything that would create division in the organizational chart. In addition, individuals they appointed would be in danger of being seen as spies, which would break down trust within the organization.

The issue was resolved right before the end of negotiations: the number of positions, how the process would work, and the right to terminate and review. If I fired someone, everyone realized, the Chinese counterpart would lose face. So I had to provide performance evaluations to the Chinese company and give them the chance to replace somebody who wasn't performing by nominating someone else.

The path became much easier once everyone understood that we weren't going to get the deal done unless we allowed the Chinese to be a part of the process from design to build to operation.

The reality is that there are always individuals who want to have a closer opportunity to connect and have oversight of business operations. A role called deputy general manager exists in many Western and Chinese joint ventures to achieve that, simply because the Chinese government or state-owned entities, or even private entities, want to have the ability to give input to decisions around any key business-related matters.

Conclusion

For more than twenty years, I've spent the majority of my time living and traveling around the world working for two powerful and well-known companies, the Walt Disney Company and Four Seasons Hotels and Resorts. I've learned how to build brands overseas and build opportunities for companies to grow in ways that are meaningful to their long-term success.

It's been an experience packed with learning. I look back and think, "Jeez, the stuff I know now that I wish I'd known that first morning I woke up in Tokyo would fill a book." And so I set out to write the book I would have wanted to read on that first flight across the Pacific. The book of things I wish I'd known.

I wanted to share my experiences for those who might be living a similar life overseas, or about to embark on one, or even simply considering it as their next step.

There's a lot to learn—and not just about the new location. It is going to be complicated at times, and you need to understand why...and what you can do about it.

Working overseas almost always entails change, not just for individuals, but also for their families and their whole businesses. Change is scary, so it is usually met with some resistance. Sometimes, the people across the table from you are not your major challenge. Sometimes it's more important to explain to your colleagues how change may impact your existing business and why it's necessary.

If a business is used to being successful doing things a certain way, it's normal to assume that way will work no matter where you go. That's far from being true, and that's one of the biggest changes the leader of any deal has to embrace: doing what's right in the particular geography.

That's hard work and relies on observation, advice, and personal experience. It relies on building trusted relationships with local partners. It relies on constant communication with the broader business.

It will bring personal pressure. Not only will you be living in a new culture. You risk being perceived as going rogue. You risk being challenged about why you're proposing to do business differently or to change the strategic partnerships. You risk sticking your neck out to alter the formula on which the company's success has been based in order to make your product or service more compelling.

You'll juggle demands from your counterparts, expectations from your employers, and above all the needs of your team in terms of support, information, and air cover. You'll juggle your personal life with your professional life in a place far removed from the place you call home.

But it's worth it, because it offers a possibility of professional success and cultural immersion that can shape not just your life but those of your colleagues, your family, your company, and everyone else connected to it. It offers a chance to build advocacy and increase understanding. And often it offers the opportunity to shape a new future for your business.

There's one more thing that often gets overlooked. Sometimes it's fine to just decide not to do the deal. That's part of what leadership is about.

Like poker players say, "You have to know when to hold 'em and know when to fold 'em."

As you get to know your deal partner, you soon come to determine whether you can align your goals with their goals and your customs and culture with their customs and culture. Most of the time it's fine, but sometimes it's not.

If it can't work, don't push it. Because in the end, I've seen businesses from multinationals to small companies close down factories or shutter outlets when they were convinced they had a successful formula for doing business everywhere but eventually had to realize that it wasn't the right time for their product or service to be part of the fabric of a particular society or geography.

Not everything will work everywhere. It takes courage to say that, because you want to do your best with the mission you've been given to negotiate a deal or run a particular region. You want the ultimate outcome to be one that your boss or your board really wants to have happen.

But if you can tell them a story in a professional and compelling fashion, backed up with facts and figures, you can enable them to understand why doing a deal or even having a presence in a particular geography may not be the right thing at the time.

It doesn't mean it might not be right in the future. Opportunities come around again as societies or cultures evolve, as happened in China. As more people there became income qualified, they also became more sophisticated in their understanding of Western culture. The Chinese government came to understand that products related to leisure and tourism would better the quality of life of their citizens rather than simply create jobs like manufacturing plants do.

When they finally decided to act, that was the right time for Disney or Four Seasons or other companies in those fields to throw themselves into the market. When you have a product or service that is compelling enough, you'll be ready to take advantage of the timing.

And that's the most important lesson of all. Whatever happens, be ready.

Acknowledgments

Thank you to the teams who dedicated themselves to a vision of success that sometimes seemed unattainable! Your belief, drive, and willingness to just "do what needed to be done" is something that will never be forgotten. You are all my friends, and I'm proud to have worked alongside you to make the magic happen! Every leader should be so lucky!!

About the Author

MICHAEL CRAWFORD is the Chairman of the Board, President and Chief Executive Officer for Hall of Fame Resort & Entertainment Company and its subsidiaries, including Hall of Fame Village powered by Johnson Controls, which he joined in December of 2018. An Ohio native, he holds an undergraduate degree from Bowling Green State University and a master's degree in business administration from the University of Notre Dame. He brings to the company demonstrated leadership experience from his development of retail and dining establishments, hotels, theme parks, and entertainment destinations around the world. Prior to leading Hall of Fame Resort & Entertainment Company, Mr. Crawford spent four years with the Four Seasons Hotels and Resorts Company. He started as President of Asia Pacific and went on to become Global President of Portfolio Management. While at Four Seasons, Mr. Crawford led a company repositioning effort in Asia and oversaw all hotel development and operations for the region. Prior to that, Mr. Crawford spent almost twenty-five years at the Walt Disney Company. He rose to Senior Vice President and General Manager of Shanghai Disney Resort and President of Shanghai's Walt Disney Holdings Company. Mr. Crawford led the negotiation and multi-billion-dollar development of Shanghai Disney Resort from 2007–2014. Mr. Crawford also currently serves as a member of the Board of Directors for Texas Roadhouse. Mr. Crawford and his wife, Kim, enjoy traveling, hiking, playing golf, and spending time with his daughter, Kaitlin, who graduated from the University of Notre Dame in 2020, and now resides and works in Boise, Idaho as a wilderness therapist supervisor while also pursuing her master's degree in public health from Tulane University.